Debt-for-Nature Swaps: Financial Solutions for Sustainability and Climate Action

I0119063

Copyright

Debt-for-Nature Swaps: Financial Solutions for Sustainability and Climate Action

© 2025 Robert C. Brears

Published by Global Climate Solutions

ISBN (eBook): 978-1-991369-15-4

ISBN (Paperback): 978-1-991369-16-1

Table of Contents

Preface

In an era where the twin crises of sovereign debt and environmental degradation threaten global stability, debt-for-nature swaps have emerged as a transformative financial tool. These innovative agreements offer indebted nations the opportunity to redirect financial resources from debt repayment toward crucial environmental conservation and climate resilience efforts. By leveraging financial relief for ecological preservation, these swaps create a bridge between economic stability and sustainable development.

The concept of debt-for-nature swaps is not new; its origins date back to the 1980s when environmental organizations and international financial institutions recognized the potential of linking debt reduction with conservation efforts. Over time, these mechanisms have evolved, incorporating new financial instruments, technological advancements, and broader climate-related objectives. Today, they stand as a vital tool in the global push for sustainable development, aligning with international frameworks such as the Paris Agreement and the United Nations Sustainable Development Goals (SDGs).

This book explores the intricacies of debt-for-nature swaps, detailing their mechanics, historical evolution, key stakeholders, and modern applications. It examines how these agreements have been adapted to address climate change mitigation and adaptation, enhance biodiversity conservation, and promote economic stability in developing nations. Additionally, it highlights the role of technological innovations—such as blockchain, GIS, and satellite monitoring—in ensuring transparency, accountability, and effectiveness in implementation.

By delving into the strategic, financial, and environmental dimensions of debt-for-nature swaps, this book provides a comprehensive guide for policymakers, financial institutions, conservation organizations, and researchers. The insights presented aim to foster a deeper understanding of how these financial instruments can be leveraged to achieve both economic relief and ecological resilience in an increasingly interconnected world.

As we navigate the challenges of climate change and financial instability, debt-for-nature swaps offer a pathway toward a sustainable and equitable future. This book serves as a resource for those seeking to harness their potential in shaping global environmental and economic policy.

Chapter 1: Introduction to Debt-for-Nature Swaps

Debt-for-nature swaps are a unique financial tool that offers a solution to the intertwined challenges of sovereign debt and environmental degradation. By linking debt relief with environmental conservation, these swaps allow countries to reduce their external debt burdens while simultaneously investing in the preservation of critical ecosystems. This chapter provides an introduction to the concept of debt-for-nature swaps, exploring their origins, how they work, and the key stakeholders involved. It sets the stage for understanding the potential of these swaps as a tool for sustainable development and environmental protection in the context of global financial challenges.

1.1 Defining Debt-for-Nature Swaps

Debt-for-nature swaps are an innovative financial tool designed to simultaneously address the pressing issues of sovereign debt and environmental degradation. By linking the reduction of a country's sovereign debt with a commitment to invest in environmental conservation, debt-for-nature swaps create a mutually beneficial arrangement for debtor countries, creditors, and environmental stakeholders. These swaps involve the forgiveness or purchase of external debt in exchange for commitments to fund conservation efforts, sustainable resource management, and other environmentally-focused programs. This section outlines the concept of debt-for-nature swaps, their historical development, key milestones, and their role in sustainable development.

Overview of the Debt-for-Nature Swap Concept

The basic principle behind debt-for-nature swaps is straightforward: a creditor (usually a developed country or international financial institution) agrees to forgive a portion of the debt owed by a developing country, provided the debtor country commits to using the equivalent amount of money for environmental conservation. In some variations of the swap, a third-party organization, such as an environmental NGO, may purchase the debt at a discount and then negotiate with the debtor government to allocate the debt forgiveness towards conservation efforts. The funds freed by debt reduction are typically directed to activities such as protecting biodiversity, promoting sustainable agriculture, establishing protected areas, or supporting reforestation programs.

The idea is to provide debtor countries with financial relief while simultaneously addressing critical environmental challenges, particularly in regions that are rich in biodiversity but face economic pressures. By creating this linkage between debt relief and environmental protection, debt-for-nature swaps align financial goals with ecological sustainability, ensuring that countries can reduce their debt burden while making long-term investments in the preservation of their natural resources.

Historical Development and Key Milestones

The origins of debt-for-nature swaps can be traced back to the early 1980s when many developing countries, particularly in Latin America, were experiencing a debt crisis. At the same time, these countries were home to some of the world's most ecologically significant ecosystems, such as tropical rainforests, coral reefs, and wetlands, that were being threatened by overexploitation. Debt-for-nature swaps were proposed as a means of alleviating the debt burden of these countries while also promoting conservation efforts.

The first formal debt-for-nature swap took place in 1987 between Bolivia and the United States, in which the U.S. government agreed to forgive $650 million of Bolivia's debt in exchange for the country's commitment to use the equivalent amount of money for environmental protection, particularly the conservation of its Amazon rainforest. This agreement, facilitated by the U.S. Treasury and environmental organizations like The Nature Conservancy, marked a milestone in the development of debt-for-nature swaps and demonstrated that such arrangements could be used to address both financial and environmental crises.

Following Bolivia's example, other countries, particularly in Latin America, adopted debt-for-nature swaps. Costa Rica, for example, entered into a debt-for-nature swap agreement in 1989, which led to the creation of new national parks and reforestation programs. The success of these early initiatives inspired additional agreements in the 1990s and 2000s, including swaps in countries such as the Philippines, Madagascar, and Senegal. Over time, the debt-for-nature swap concept gained broader acceptance and evolved into a formal tool for debt relief and environmental protection, with international financial institutions like the World Bank becoming more involved in facilitating swaps and providing technical assistance.

Role of Debt-for-Nature Swaps in Sustainable Development

Debt-for-nature swaps play an essential role in sustainable development by addressing both economic and environmental challenges simultaneously. In many developing countries, the burden of external debt restricts the ability of governments to allocate resources to essential social programs, including those aimed at environmental conservation. By providing financial relief, debt-for-nature swaps free up resources that can be reinvested in the protection of natural resources, helping countries achieve a more balanced and sustainable form of development.

Debt-for-nature swaps align with the broader goals of sustainable development by supporting efforts to preserve biodiversity, combat climate change, and protect ecosystems that provide critical services such as clean water, food, and carbon sequestration. These swaps contribute to the achievement of the United Nations Sustainable Development Goals (SDGs), particularly Goal 15 (Life on Land) and Goal 14 (Life Below Water), which focus on the conservation of terrestrial and marine ecosystems, respectively. By financing conservation efforts through debt reduction, these swaps offer a practical way to integrate environmental sustainability into national development plans while reducing the pressures associated with sovereign debt.

Furthermore, debt-for-nature swaps have a positive impact on local communities by promoting sustainable livelihoods, particularly in areas where natural resources are critical to the economy. For example, initiatives funded through debt-for-nature swaps can support ecotourism, sustainable agriculture, and community-based conservation, providing long-term economic benefits while protecting the environment. In this way, debt-for-nature swaps contribute to both poverty reduction and environmental preservation, fostering a more sustainable future for countries with limited resources.

Debt-for-nature swaps have emerged as a unique and effective mechanism for addressing the challenges of sovereign debt and environmental degradation. By providing debtor countries with the financial relief needed to prioritize conservation and sustainable development, these swaps contribute to the long-term health of ecosystems and the achievement of global sustainability goals. The historical development of debt-for-nature swaps, beginning with the 1987 Bolivia-U.S. agreement, has set the stage for their widespread use in the 21st century, positioning them as a vital tool for achieving both economic stability and environmental sustainability in developing nations.

1.2 The Need for Debt-for-Nature Swaps

Debt-for-nature swaps arise from the confluence of two critical global challenges: sovereign debt crises in developing countries and escalating environmental degradation. As developing nations struggle with mounting debt, their capacity to address pressing environmental issues is severely constrained. At the same time, the economic costs of biodiversity loss and environmental damage continue to increase. Debt-for-nature swaps offer an integrated solution to both crises, providing countries with much-needed debt relief while simultaneously funding essential environmental protection efforts. This section explores the reasons behind the need for debt-for-nature swaps and how they serve as a mechanism for tackling both financial and ecological challenges.

Sovereign Debt Crises in Developing Countries

Sovereign debt crises are a recurring issue in many developing countries, particularly those in Latin America, Africa, and Asia. In the 1980s and 1990s, many countries in the Global South faced crippling debt burdens, exacerbated by poor economic conditions, external shocks, and ineffective financial management. These countries were often forced to divert limited resources to servicing debt, leaving little room to invest in essential public services, including environmental conservation.

For many developing nations, the external debt is compounded by unfavorable lending terms, such as high interest rates and short repayment periods, which increase the burden on their economies. As the debt grows, countries face diminishing fiscal flexibility, leading to social instability and economic hardship. In these circumstances, environmental conservation becomes a lower priority as governments are forced to focus on meeting immediate debt obligations, often at the expense of long-term sustainability. Deforestation, resource depletion, and pollution increase as governments turn to unsustainable economic practices to generate revenue.

Debt-for-nature swaps directly address this issue by offering a way for debtor countries to reduce their debt burden while simultaneously making investments in environmental sustainability. By linking debt relief with conservation efforts, these swaps enable countries to prioritize long-term ecological goals without sacrificing economic stability.

Environmental Degradation and the Economic Cost of Biodiversity Loss

Environmental degradation, particularly biodiversity loss, presents a significant challenge to developing countries. Many nations in the Global South are home to some of the world's most important and biodiverse ecosystems, including tropical rainforests, coral reefs, and wetlands. However, these ecosystems are increasingly under threat from activities such as deforestation, mining, agriculture, and urbanization. The degradation of these ecosystems not only threatens biodiversity but also undermines the livelihoods of local communities that depend on natural resources for agriculture, fishing, and tourism.

The economic costs of environmental damage are often overlooked but are significant. For instance, the loss of forests can lead to soil erosion, reduced water quality, and a decline in agricultural productivity. Similarly, the destruction of coral reefs reduces fish populations, affecting local fisheries and food security. The depletion of natural resources also diminishes a country's ability to generate sustainable revenue in the long run, further hindering its economic development.

The loss of biodiversity also has global consequences, as ecosystems provide critical services such as carbon sequestration, water purification, and climate regulation. The economic cost of this loss is substantial, both for individual countries and for the global community. Addressing these environmental challenges requires substantial investment, but many developing countries lack the financial resources to fund such efforts. This is where debt-for-nature swaps become essential, as they provide a mechanism for generating the funds necessary for conservation while alleviating the burden of debt.

How Debt-for-Nature Swaps Serve as an Integrated Solution

Debt-for-nature swaps present an integrated solution to the challenges of sovereign debt and environmental degradation by addressing both issues simultaneously. The concept behind these swaps is simple yet innovative: a creditor agrees to forgive or reduce a portion of a debtor country's debt in exchange for the country's commitment to invest the money saved into environmental conservation. This allows debtor countries to relieve some of the pressure from their financial obligations while also funding conservation programs that can help protect and restore vital ecosystems.

Debt-for-nature swaps are particularly beneficial for countries rich in natural resources but facing significant debt burdens. The funds released through debt relief can be used to establish protected areas, promote sustainable land management practices, support reforestation projects, and combat illegal logging or poaching. These efforts help preserve biodiversity and ecosystem services that are essential for long-term economic stability. Additionally, by fostering a relationship between financial relief and environmental protection, debt-for-nature swaps create a more sustainable model of development that takes into account both economic and ecological needs.

Moreover, these swaps can generate a positive feedback loop, where the environmental benefits lead to improved economic outcomes. For example, protecting forests and establishing wildlife reserves can boost ecotourism, create jobs, and generate long-term revenue streams. Similarly, sustainable agriculture and land management practices can increase agricultural productivity and food security. By investing in the environment, countries not only reduce their debt but also build the foundation for a more resilient and sustainable economy.

In summary, debt-for-nature swaps offer a unique and integrated solution to the pressing issues of sovereign debt and environmental degradation. These swaps provide financial relief while also enabling countries to address critical environmental challenges, making them a vital tool for achieving sustainable development in the Global South. Through these innovative agreements, debt relief and conservation go hand in hand, fostering a more sustainable future for both economies and ecosystems.

1.3 Stakeholders in Debt-for-Nature Swaps

Debt-for-nature swaps involve a variety of stakeholders, each playing a crucial role in the negotiation, implementation, and success of these agreements. The main stakeholders in debt-for-nature swaps include governments of both debtor and creditor nations, non-governmental organizations (NGOs), creditors, and the private sector. Each group has distinct responsibilities and incentives that drive their participation in these swaps. This section outlines the role of these stakeholders and their respective responsibilities and incentives.

Role of Governments

Governments are at the heart of debt-for-nature swaps, as they represent the debtor country that seeks relief from sovereign debt while committing to environmental conservation. The government of the debtor country negotiates with creditors to secure debt reduction in exchange for the commitment to fund specific environmental initiatives, such as establishing protected areas, promoting sustainable agriculture, or implementing reforestation projects. The role of the debtor government is to ensure that the funds released from debt relief are allocated effectively toward these conservation goals.

The government also plays a critical role in ensuring that the conditions of the swap are met and that the funds are used transparently for their intended purposes. In many cases, the debtor country's government may need to create or strengthen institutions to manage the funds, such as an environmental trust fund, and to monitor the progress of conservation projects.

On the creditor side, governments play a pivotal role in the decision-making process, as they may be the direct holders of the debt or involved through multilateral institutions. In the context of bilateral swaps, creditor governments, often through diplomatic channels, agree to forgive a portion of the debtor's debt in exchange for the environmental commitments. In multilateral swaps, the government's role is typically more indirect, with the creditor working through international financial institutions to facilitate the debt reduction process.

Role of NGOs

NGOs are key actors in the design and execution of debt-for-nature swaps. They are often responsible for providing technical expertise on environmental conservation, monitoring the allocation and use of funds, and ensuring that the environmental goals of the swap are met. NGOs like The Nature Conservancy, WWF, and other specialized environmental organizations frequently act as intermediaries, helping broker the deal between the debtor country and creditors. They are often involved in the assessment of the country's environmental needs, recommending projects for funding, and providing on-the-ground expertise during the implementation phase.

The incentives for NGOs to participate in debt-for-nature swaps are primarily linked to their mission of environmental protection. Through these swaps, NGOs can achieve tangible conservation outcomes by securing funding for crucial projects that they may otherwise not have the resources to implement. Furthermore, NGOs benefit from the visibility and legitimacy that debt-for-nature swaps can provide, as they are often seen as playing an essential role in both securing financial relief and achieving positive environmental impacts.

Additionally, NGOs may help ensure that the benefits of the swap extend to local communities. By facilitating community-based conservation programs and promoting sustainable livelihoods, they can contribute to the broader social goals of these initiatives, such as poverty reduction and improving community engagement in environmental protection.

Role of Creditors

Creditors, often government institutions or international financial organizations, are central to debt-for-nature swaps. Their role is to agree to forgive a portion of the debtor's outstanding debt in exchange for a commitment to fund environmental initiatives. Creditors are typically involved in the negotiation process, working with the debtor country and NGOs to determine the scope of the swap and the environmental outcomes that will be achieved. In many cases, creditors may also set conditions for the swap, such as ensuring that the funds are used for specific projects or that the conservation efforts are aligned with international environmental goals.

For creditors, the incentives to participate in debt-for-nature swaps are both financial and diplomatic. Reducing sovereign debt through swaps can help alleviate the debt burden of developing nations, which may reduce the likelihood of default and stabilize international financial markets. Additionally, for creditor governments, debt-for-nature swaps can be seen as a means to enhance diplomatic relations and promote global environmental goals, such as the protection of biodiversity and the mitigation of climate change. They may also serve to demonstrate commitment to sustainability, thereby aligning with domestic and international environmental policies.

Role of the Private Sector

In recent years, the private sector has become increasingly involved in debt-for-nature swaps, both as a source of funding and as a partner in implementing conservation projects. Private sector companies, particularly those involved in industries that rely on natural resources, such as agriculture, forestry, and mining, have a vested interest in sustainable resource management. Their role in debt-for-nature swaps may include providing funding through impact investing or corporate social responsibility (CSR) initiatives, which are focused on environmental sustainability.

For companies, the incentives to participate in debt-for-nature swaps are often related to their need to mitigate environmental risks that could impact their operations and supply chains. For instance, companies that rely on forest products may support reforestation or sustainable forestry initiatives to ensure a stable supply of resources. Similarly, companies in the extractive industries may support biodiversity conservation to help maintain ecosystem services that benefit their operations, such as water purification or climate regulation.

Private sector involvement in debt-for-nature swaps also provides companies with an opportunity to align with global sustainability goals, enhance their corporate image, and engage in long-term environmental stewardship. Through participation in these swaps, they can not only contribute to the preservation of natural resources but also reduce their exposure to environmental risks and improve their overall sustainability credentials.

Debt-for-nature swaps rely on the active participation of a diverse group of stakeholders, including governments, NGOs, creditors, and the private sector. Each of these parties brings unique responsibilities and incentives to the table, working together to achieve the dual goals of reducing sovereign debt and promoting environmental sustainability. Governments negotiate the terms of the swap and ensure the funds are directed to conservation, while NGOs provide technical expertise and ensure that the conservation goals are met. Creditors participate to reduce debt risk and promote international environmental goals, and the private sector engages to ensure resource sustainability and align with corporate social responsibility initiatives. Through these partnerships, debt-for-nature swaps offer a multifaceted solution to the pressing financial and environmental challenges faced by developing countries.

Chapter 2: The Mechanics of Debt-for-Nature Swaps

Understanding how debt-for-nature swaps function is essential to appreciating their role in addressing both sovereign debt and environmental degradation. This chapter explores the step-by-step mechanics of debt-for-nature swaps, examining the financial arrangements, key negotiations, and operational processes that make these agreements successful. By diving into the specific mechanisms that drive debt-for-nature swaps, we will highlight how these deals are structured and the various ways they ensure funds are allocated effectively to achieve long-term conservation goals.

2.1 How Debt-for-Nature Swaps Work

Debt-for-nature swaps involve a series of steps designed to reduce sovereign debt while simultaneously financing environmental conservation projects. These swaps are structured agreements between debtor countries, creditors, and third-party organizations like NGOs that result in the forgiveness of debt in exchange for environmental commitments. This section outlines the step-by-step process of a debt-for-nature swap, the key financial mechanisms involved, and the management of conservation projects funded by the agreement.

Step-by-Step Process of a Debt-for-Nature Swap

1. Identifying Debt and Environmental Objectives

The process begins when a debtor country, usually a developing nation facing significant external debt, approaches creditors and relevant stakeholders with a proposal for a debt-for-nature swap. The first step is identifying the amount of debt to be reduced and the specific environmental objectives to be achieved. The government of the debtor country, along with environmental NGOs and experts, conducts an assessment of its environmental priorities, such as protecting biodiversity, conserving forests, or restoring degraded ecosystems. The debtor country and creditor work together to define which conservation projects will be funded by the debt relief.

2. Negotiation of Terms

Once the environmental goals are established, the next step is the negotiation of terms between the debtor country and the creditor. These negotiations determine the amount of debt to be forgiven and the conditions tied to the swap. The debtor agrees to allocate funds that would have been used for debt repayment toward conservation projects. Typically, the creditor country agrees to forgive a portion of the debt in exchange for the debtor country's commitment to environmental objectives. In some cases, a third-party organization, such as The Nature Conservancy, may facilitate the negotiation and provide technical support for structuring the swap.

3. Debt Purchase or Reduction

In some cases, debt-for-nature swaps involve the purchase of debt at a discounted rate. NGOs or private entities may purchase the debt from the creditor, usually at a fraction of its face value, which reduces the total amount of debt owed by the debtor country. The difference between the discounted purchase price and the face value of the debt is forgiven, with the amount of debt relief tied to specific conservation commitments. Alternatively, the creditor may agree to reduce the debt directly without involving third-party purchases.

4. Establishing a Trust Fund or Financial Mechanism

Once the debt reduction is agreed upon, a trust fund or financial mechanism is established to manage the funds freed from debt repayment. This fund is responsible for ensuring that the money saved from debt relief is allocated to specific conservation projects. Often, this fund is managed by a joint board consisting of representatives from the debtor country, the creditor, and conservation organizations. The trust fund provides a transparent and accountable way to manage and disburse the funds for conservation initiatives.

5. Implementation of Conservation Projects

With the funds in place, the next step is the implementation of conservation projects. These projects may involve creating protected areas, establishing national parks, reforestation efforts, sustainable land management programs, or wildlife conservation initiatives. NGOs, along with the debtor country's government, typically take the lead in implementing these projects, often working with local communities to ensure their success. The involvement of local communities is crucial to ensuring that the projects are sustainable and aligned with the needs of the people living in or near the conservation areas.

6. Monitoring and Reporting

To ensure that the conservation projects are effective, continuous monitoring and reporting are essential. NGOs, often with the assistance of international organizations, monitor the progress of conservation initiatives and ensure that the funds are being used appropriately. Regular reports are submitted to stakeholders, including the creditor, debtor government, and environmental organizations, detailing the progress of the conservation projects. This transparency helps ensure accountability and provides an opportunity to make adjustments to the projects if necessary.

Key Financial Mechanisms Involved

The financial mechanisms involved in debt-for-nature swaps are designed to convert a portion of sovereign debt into funding for environmental conservation. The key financial mechanisms include debt forgiveness, debt purchase, and the establishment of a conservation trust fund.

1. Debt Forgiveness

Debt forgiveness is the primary financial mechanism in a debt-for-nature swap. A creditor agrees to forgive a portion of the debt owed by the debtor country in exchange for a commitment to use the equivalent amount of savings for environmental projects. This reduction in debt can provide significant financial relief for debtor countries and free up resources for conservation and sustainable development initiatives.

2. Debt Purchase at a Discount

Another financial mechanism is the purchase of debt at a discounted rate by a third-party organization, such as an environmental NGO or a private entity. For example, if a debtor country owes $100 million, a third party might purchase the debt for $60 million. The debtor country then benefits from a reduction in its total debt, and the environmental organization is able to use the remaining funds for conservation programs. This mechanism allows for an immediate reduction in debt while ensuring that a substantial portion of the debt savings is invested in environmental protection.

3. Conservation Trust Fund

A conservation trust fund is often established as part of the financial structure of a debt-for-nature swap. The trust fund is responsible for managing the funds released through debt reduction and ensuring that they are used effectively for conservation initiatives. The trust fund typically includes representatives from the debtor country, the creditor, and environmental organizations, and it helps to guarantee transparency and accountability in the use of funds. The fund may also include long-term financial mechanisms, such as endowment funds or revenue-generating activities, to ensure the sustainability of conservation efforts.

Managing and Overseeing Conservation Projects

The management and oversight of conservation projects funded through debt-for-nature swaps are critical to their success. Effective governance structures are necessary to ensure that the funds are used as intended and that the environmental goals are achieved. NGOs often play a central role in managing the projects, providing technical expertise, and ensuring that the programs are implemented successfully.

The governance of conservation projects typically involves setting clear environmental targets and performance indicators. Monitoring the progress of the projects is essential for ensuring that the funds are being used efficiently and that the projects are achieving the desired outcomes. Independent audits and evaluations may also be conducted periodically to assess the effectiveness of the conservation initiatives and identify areas for improvement.

Furthermore, the involvement of local communities is essential in ensuring the long-term sustainability of the projects. By engaging local populations in the planning, implementation, and management of conservation efforts, debt-for-nature swaps can contribute to the development of sustainable livelihoods and foster a sense of ownership over the conservation programs.

In summary, the process of debt-for-nature swaps involves several stages, including negotiation, debt reduction, establishment of a trust fund, implementation of conservation projects, and ongoing monitoring. The financial mechanisms at play, such as debt forgiveness and debt purchase, ensure that resources are freed up for environmental projects. Effective management and oversight of these projects, combined with the involvement of local communities and NGOs, are essential for the long-term success of debt-for-nature swaps.

2.2 Financial Arrangements in Debt-for-Nature Swaps

Debt-for-nature swaps involve complex financial arrangements designed to alleviate the debt burdens of developing nations while providing funds for environmental conservation. These agreements generally take two forms: debt forgiveness and debt purchase, both of which have distinct mechanisms and financial implications. In addition, the establishment of conservation trust funds plays a key role in managing the resources freed through debt reduction, ensuring that they are effectively used for conservation goals. This section examines the various financial mechanisms at play, including debt forgiveness versus debt purchase, the role of conservation trust funds, and risk-sharing mechanisms in debt-for-nature swaps.

Debt Forgiveness vs. Debt Purchase

The two primary financial mechanisms involved in debt-for-nature swaps are debt forgiveness and debt purchase. Each has distinct processes and implications for the debtor country, creditor, and conservation organizations.

1. Debt Forgiveness

Debt forgiveness involves the partial or total cancellation of sovereign debt, typically agreed upon by the debtor country and the creditor. In a debt-for-nature swap, a creditor (such as a government or international financial institution) agrees to forgive a portion of the debt owed by the debtor country, contingent upon the debtor's commitment to invest the equivalent amount in environmental conservation programs. This agreement directly reduces the total debt burden of the debtor country, freeing up resources that can be used for conservation initiatives.

Debt forgiveness is often negotiated between the governments of the creditor and debtor countries, along with international organizations or environmental NGOs. This mechanism is particularly useful when the debtor country's debt is unsustainable and it faces significant financial strain. By forgiving the debt, creditors aim to promote stability and economic recovery in debtor nations while contributing to environmental goals, such as protecting biodiversity, forest ecosystems, or freshwater resources. The main advantage of debt forgiveness is that it provides immediate financial relief to the debtor country, reducing fiscal pressures and allowing for the redirection of funds toward conservation.

2. **Debt Purchase**

In contrast to debt forgiveness, debt purchase involves an intermediary, often an environmental NGO, purchasing the debt at a discounted rate from the creditor. For example, if a debtor country owes $100 million in debt, an NGO or environmental organization may purchase it for $60 million, thus forgiving the remaining $40 million of debt. This purchase agreement effectively reduces the debtor country's debt by a substantial amount while ensuring that the environmental organization can use the savings for conservation activities. Debt purchase is typically conducted at a significant discount, providing creditors with an immediate financial gain by selling the debt at below-market value.

Debt purchase may involve both public and private sector actors, with NGOs often acting as intermediaries in the process. This mechanism is particularly advantageous when the creditor is willing to sell debt at a discount and when there is sufficient capacity within the environmental organization to manage the funds for conservation. Debt purchase arrangements may also be easier to structure in cases where debt forgiveness by the creditor is politically challenging or where there is a need for a third-party facilitator to ensure that conservation goals are met.

Role of Conservation Trust Funds and Other Financing Structures

Once the debt is forgiven or purchased, the next critical financial arrangement is the establishment of a conservation trust fund or similar financing structure. These funds are set up to manage and allocate the resources freed from debt relief to specific conservation projects. A conservation trust fund serves as a dedicated pool of funds that is used to finance long-term environmental protection initiatives, such as the establishment of protected areas, reforestation programs, or biodiversity conservation.

Conservation trust funds are typically managed by a board of trustees, which may include representatives from the debtor government, the creditor, and environmental NGOs. The trust fund ensures that funds are used transparently and for their intended purpose, with mechanisms in place for oversight and accountability. It also allows for the long-term management of funds, ensuring that the conservation initiatives funded by the swap can continue to receive financial support in the future.

The establishment of such funds is critical to the success of debt-for-nature swaps, as they provide a transparent and sustainable way to manage the resources freed from debt reduction. In some cases, these funds may also include revenue-generating mechanisms, such as ecotourism fees or payments for ecosystem services, which can help supplement the financial resources available for conservation.

Risk-Sharing Mechanisms

Risk-sharing mechanisms are an important aspect of the financial arrangements in debt-for-nature swaps. These mechanisms are designed to reduce the financial risks faced by both the creditor and the debtor country, ensuring that both parties are incentivized to participate in the swap. Risk-sharing mechanisms typically involve the use of insurance, guarantees, or other financial instruments to mitigate the risks associated with conservation projects and the implementation of debt-for-nature swaps.

1. **Insurance**

One of the most common risk-sharing mechanisms in debt-for-nature swaps is the use of insurance products, which protect both the debtor country and the creditor against the financial risks associated with environmental conservation projects. Insurance can cover various risks, such as the failure of conservation projects to meet their objectives, political instability, or unforeseen environmental events like natural disasters that may disrupt conservation efforts. By providing insurance, both parties are assured that they will not be financially exposed if the swap does not achieve its intended outcomes.

2. **Guarantees**

Another risk-sharing mechanism involves guarantees, where a third party, often an international financial institution or development bank, provides a guarantee that the debtor country will meet its environmental commitments. These guarantees can be used to back the funds allocated for conservation, providing creditors with assurance that the funds will be properly managed and used for their intended purpose. Guarantees can also be used to reduce the perceived risk of entering into debt-for-nature swaps, particularly in countries with weak financial or governance systems.

3. **Blended Finance**

Blended finance is another approach to risk-sharing, where public funds are used to leverage private sector investment in conservation. In a blended finance arrangement, public and philanthropic funds are used to reduce risks and attract private capital, making it easier for private investors to participate in debt-for-nature swaps. This approach allows for larger-scale conservation projects, as private investors are more willing to invest in initiatives that have a lower risk profile. Blended finance can also help mobilize additional resources for conservation, allowing debt-for-nature swaps to have a broader impact.

In summary, the financial arrangements involved in debt-for-nature swaps are complex but essential to their success. Debt forgiveness and debt purchase are the primary mechanisms used to reduce sovereign debt, while conservation trust funds provide a transparent way to manage funds for long-term environmental projects. Risk-sharing mechanisms, such as insurance, guarantees, and blended finance, help to mitigate the risks associated with these swaps and encourage participation from both creditors and debtor countries. Together, these financial structures create a sustainable framework for leveraging debt reduction to support critical conservation efforts around the world.

2.3 Long-Term Monitoring and Accountability

Monitoring and accountability are crucial components of debt-for-nature swaps, ensuring that the funds released through debt reduction are used effectively for environmental conservation. Without robust mechanisms to track the allocation and impact of these funds, there is a risk that the intended environmental goals may not be achieved. This section outlines the processes involved in monitoring and managing funds, the role of NGOs and third-party organizations in ensuring compliance, and the technological tools that facilitate tracking and reporting progress.

How Funds are Monitored and Managed

Once the debt-for-nature swap agreement is in place and the funds have been allocated for conservation projects, it is essential to establish clear mechanisms to monitor and manage these resources. The management of funds typically involves the creation of a dedicated conservation trust fund or financial management structure, which is responsible for overseeing the use of the funds. These trust funds are designed to ensure that the money saved from debt reduction is directed exclusively to environmental conservation initiatives.

To ensure proper fund management, transparent financial systems are put in place to track the allocation and disbursement of funds. These systems help prevent corruption and misuse of funds by maintaining an open and accessible record of financial transactions. Often, the funds are divided into various categories or projects, such as reforestation, sustainable land management, or the creation of protected areas, each of which is monitored to ensure that the projects remain on track and meet their conservation targets.

The government of the debtor country is usually responsible for implementing the conservation projects, but they are often supported by independent financial experts and environmental organizations to ensure proper fund management. These professionals help ensure that the funds are used efficiently and in accordance with the agreed-upon conservation goals. Additionally, regular audits and reviews are typically conducted to verify the use of the funds and ensure compliance with the terms of the debt-for-nature swap agreement.

Role of NGOs and Third-Party Organizations in Ensuring Compliance

NGOs and third-party organizations play a vital role in the monitoring and management of conservation funds. These organizations are often involved from the outset, helping to negotiate the terms of the debt-for-nature swap and ensuring that the environmental goals are clearly defined. Once the agreement is in place, NGOs typically assist in implementing the conservation projects, providing technical expertise, and overseeing the day-to-day management of the funds.

One of the key roles of NGOs is to act as independent monitors, ensuring that the funds are being used for the intended conservation purposes. NGOs provide valuable oversight, ensuring that conservation efforts are not only effective but also sustainable in the long term. This independent oversight is essential in maintaining the credibility of the debt-for-nature swap, as it assures stakeholders— including creditors, debtor governments, and the public—that the funds are being used as intended.

In many cases, NGOs also work to ensure compliance with the broader goals of the swap, such as protecting biodiversity or promoting sustainable development. They may engage with local communities to ensure that the projects meet their needs and that they are involved in the conservation process. NGOs are also critical in the evaluation of the success of conservation initiatives, providing reports and recommendations to ensure that projects are on track and that any obstacles are addressed promptly.

Third-party organizations such as international development banks or environmental foundations often serve as neutral parties in debt-for-nature swaps, providing additional oversight and ensuring that both the creditor and the debtor country comply with the terms of the agreement. These organizations help maintain transparency in the use of funds, which is crucial for ensuring the legitimacy and effectiveness of the swap.

Technological Tools for Tracking Progress

Advancements in technology have significantly improved the ability to monitor the progress of conservation projects funded through debt-for-nature swaps. Technological tools such as Geographic Information Systems (GIS), satellite imagery, and blockchain are increasingly being used to track the use of funds and assess the environmental impact of conservation efforts.

1. GIS

GIS technology is a powerful tool for monitoring environmental changes and the progress of conservation projects. It allows stakeholders to map out conservation areas, track changes in land use, and monitor the effectiveness of reforestation or habitat restoration efforts. GIS can also be used to track biodiversity, such as species movement, which helps to determine the success of protected areas or wildlife conservation programs. By integrating spatial data with environmental and financial data, GIS tools provide a comprehensive view of the progress of conservation efforts, allowing for real-time adjustments if necessary.

2. Satellite Imagery

Satellite imagery is another key technological tool used to track the progress of conservation projects. High-resolution satellite images allow for the monitoring of large areas of land, such as forests or protected areas, without the need for on-the-ground inspections. Satellite imagery can be used to detect changes in land cover, such as deforestation or the expansion of illegal activities like mining or logging. This technology provides an effective way to ensure that conservation projects are being implemented as planned and that funds are being used to protect critical ecosystems.

3. Blockchain Technology

Blockchain technology is being increasingly used in debt-for-nature swaps to provide transparency and accountability in the management of conservation funds. Blockchain's decentralized and immutable ledger allows for real-time tracking of financial transactions, ensuring that funds are allocated correctly and that there is no misuse. By recording every transaction in a transparent and auditable manner, blockchain provides stakeholders with a secure, verifiable record of how funds are being spent. This technology reduces the risk of corruption and ensures that funds are directed precisely to the intended conservation projects.

4. Digital Platforms for Stakeholder Engagement

Digital platforms are increasingly being used to facilitate communication among stakeholders involved in debt-for-nature swaps. These platforms allow governments, NGOs, and local communities to share information, track progress, and coordinate efforts in real time. By using online platforms, stakeholders can access up-to-date reports, environmental data, and financial information, ensuring that all parties are informed and engaged in the project. Digital platforms also allow for greater participation from local communities, as they can provide feedback, report issues, and collaborate on conservation efforts.

In conclusion, long-term monitoring and accountability are integral components of debt-for-nature swaps, ensuring that funds are effectively managed and that conservation projects meet their environmental goals. The use of independent financial oversight by NGOs, along with advanced technological tools such as GIS, satellite imagery, and blockchain, helps to ensure transparency and track the progress of conservation initiatives. These monitoring systems provide real-time data, allowing stakeholders to make adjustments and ensuring that the funds released through debt reduction are used efficiently and sustainably. Through these robust monitoring and accountability mechanisms, debt-for-nature swaps can achieve long-lasting environmental and economic benefits.

Chapter 3: Challenges in Implementing Debt-for-Nature Swaps

While debt-for-nature swaps present an innovative solution to sovereign debt crises and environmental degradation, their implementation is not without significant challenges. This chapter delves into the various obstacles that can arise when executing these agreements, including political instability, insufficient financial resources, and difficulties in managing complex conservation projects. By examining these challenges, we can better understand the barriers to success and identify strategies for overcoming them to ensure that debt-for-nature swaps achieve their intended outcomes.

3.1 Political and Institutional Challenges

Political and institutional challenges are among the most significant obstacles to the successful implementation of debt-for-nature swaps. While these agreements offer financial relief and environmental benefits, their long-term success relies heavily on political stability, effective governance, and institutional capacity. This section explores the key political and institutional challenges faced by countries engaging in debt-for-nature swaps, including the impact of political instability, the need for strong institutional frameworks to manage conservation funds, and the importance of sustained commitment to sustainability.

Political Instability and Changes in Government

Political instability is one of the most pressing challenges that can hinder the success of debt-for-nature swaps. Many countries that engage in these agreements are facing fragile political environments, often characterized by frequent changes in government, civil unrest, or weak democratic institutions. In such contexts, the continuity of long-term agreements like debt-for-nature swaps can be jeopardized, as new governments may shift priorities or abandon previous commitments.

When a country's political landscape is volatile, the commitment to environmental conservation can fluctuate. A new government may view the swap as an unfavorable or politically inconvenient arrangement and may attempt to renegotiate the terms or even abandon the swap altogether. For example, changes in leadership can lead to shifts in policy, with the new government focusing more on short-term economic growth rather than long-term environmental goals. This lack of continuity can disrupt conservation efforts and erode the effectiveness of the swap.

In countries with weak political institutions, corruption can also be a major risk. The absence of robust legal and regulatory frameworks means that environmental funds allocated through debt-for-nature swaps may not be properly managed or may be diverted for other purposes. Political instability often undermines the trust required for successful debt-for-nature swaps, as creditors, NGOs, and other stakeholders may be reluctant to engage in agreements if they fear that political shifts will undermine the long-term sustainability of the initiative.

Institutional Capacity for Managing Swaps and Conservation Funds

Another significant challenge in the successful implementation of debt-for-nature swaps is the limited institutional capacity of many debtor countries to manage the funds and conservation projects effectively. The success of these swaps depends on the ability of governments to allocate and oversee the funds, ensure transparency, and implement conservation programs. However, many countries, particularly those in the Global South, often lack the institutional infrastructure and technical expertise needed to manage such complex financial arrangements.

For example, managing large sums of money directed toward environmental projects requires specialized knowledge in both financial management and environmental conservation. If the country lacks the technical expertise or the administrative infrastructure to handle these tasks, there is a risk that funds will be misallocated, wasted, or diverted away from their intended purpose. Without well-established institutions capable of overseeing the management of conservation projects, the effectiveness of the debt-for-nature swap may be compromised.

Additionally, institutional weaknesses may make it difficult to monitor the progress of conservation projects and ensure compliance with the terms of the swap. This is particularly problematic in countries where governance structures are weak and accountability mechanisms are not robust. The lack of effective monitoring and reporting systems makes it challenging to evaluate the success of conservation efforts and determine whether the environmental objectives of the swap are being met. In some cases, weak institutional capacity may lead to delays or inefficiencies in implementing conservation programs, ultimately undermining the potential impact of the debt-for-nature swap.

Importance of Strong Governance and Commitment to Sustainability

Strong governance is critical for the successful implementation and long-term sustainability of debt-for-nature swaps. Effective governance involves not only political stability but also transparent and accountable institutions that are capable of managing both the financial and environmental components of these agreements. Countries that are able to establish clear and transparent governance structures for debt-for-nature swaps are more likely to achieve positive environmental outcomes and maintain the support of all stakeholders involved.

The success of debt-for-nature swaps also depends on the commitment to sustainability by both the government and local communities. Governments must demonstrate their dedication to environmental protection by ensuring that funds from debt relief are allocated specifically for conservation and that projects are implemented effectively. This requires a clear, long-term vision for sustainable development that integrates environmental protection with economic growth. A strong commitment to sustainability also means recognizing the role of local communities in conservation efforts, ensuring that they are actively engaged and that their needs and knowledge are considered in the planning and execution of projects.

Moreover, when a government is committed to sustainability, it is more likely to integrate environmental protection into broader national development plans, ensuring that debt-for-nature swaps become part of a larger strategy for sustainable economic growth. This commitment extends beyond the immediate project period, ensuring that conservation efforts are maintained in the long run, even after the debt reduction has been achieved.

Effective governance also involves regular monitoring, transparent reporting, and independent oversight to ensure that funds are used properly and that conservation objectives are being met. Governments must create strong frameworks for accountability to ensure that both domestic and international stakeholders trust the process and continue to support the initiative.

In conclusion, political and institutional challenges represent some of the most significant obstacles to the success of debt-for-nature swaps. Political instability and changes in government can disrupt long-term commitments to environmental conservation, while weak institutional capacity can hinder effective management and oversight of funds. Strong governance, sustained commitment to sustainability, and the development of transparent and accountable institutions are essential to ensuring that debt-for-nature swaps achieve their intended environmental outcomes. By addressing these political and institutional challenges, debtor countries can better leverage debt-for-nature swaps as a tool for achieving both financial relief and sustainable development.

3.2 Financial Sustainability of Debt-for-Nature Swaps

While debt-for-nature swaps offer an innovative solution to the dual challenges of sovereign debt and environmental degradation, ensuring their long-term financial sustainability remains a critical concern. The funds released through debt reduction are typically intended to finance environmental conservation efforts, but the adequacy of these funds in achieving long-term goals can vary. This section explores the financial sustainability of debt-for-nature swaps, discussing the adequacy of debt relief in supporting long-term conservation, the challenges of integrating these swaps into national development strategies, and strategies for ensuring ongoing financing for conservation after the swap has been implemented.

Adequacy of Debt Relief in Achieving Long-Term Conservation Goals

The primary appeal of debt-for-nature swaps is their ability to reduce a country's external debt burden while providing funds for environmental conservation. However, the amount of debt relief achieved through these swaps may not always be sufficient to fund comprehensive and sustained conservation efforts. In many cases, the amount of debt reduction is a fraction of the country's overall financial needs, and while it can provide a substantial boost to conservation initiatives, it may not be enough to cover the long-term costs of large-scale environmental protection.

For instance, while the debt-for-nature swap model can relieve immediate fiscal pressure, it is often a one-time transaction that cannot replace the ongoing need for funding to maintain and expand conservation programs. Environmental protection is a long-term commitment, and the funds freed by debt relief are typically allocated to specific projects, such as establishing protected areas or promoting reforestation. However, these initial investments may not cover the ongoing costs associated with managing conservation areas, monitoring biodiversity, and addressing emerging environmental threats.

In many cases, the amount of debt forgiven or purchased may be too small relative to the scale of the country's environmental challenges. For example, a swap might free up enough funds for initial conservation projects but may not be enough to create a fully sustainable conservation infrastructure. Without additional funding or sustainable revenue-generating mechanisms, such as ecotourism or carbon credits, the success of these projects can be limited. Ensuring the adequacy of debt relief in the context of long-term conservation goals requires careful planning and consideration of future financing needs.

Challenges of Integrating Debt-for-Nature Swaps into National Development Strategies

A significant challenge in ensuring the long-term financial sustainability of debt-for-nature swaps is integrating them into broader national development strategies. In many developing countries, environmental conservation is not always prioritized in national economic planning, which can make it difficult to maintain funding for conservation projects once the debt relief is provided.

The integration of debt-for-nature swaps into national development plans requires alignment with broader goals, such as poverty reduction, economic development, and sustainable agriculture. Countries with weak environmental governance or limited institutional capacity may struggle to embed debt-for-nature swaps within national policies. For instance, environmental projects funded through debt relief may be at risk of being overshadowed by other economic priorities, such as infrastructure development or industrialization, which can lead to a misallocation of resources.

Furthermore, the integration of debt-for-nature swaps into national strategies requires the cooperation of multiple stakeholders, including government ministries, NGOs, local communities, and the private sector. Without strong coordination between these parties, conservation goals may not be fully realized. This challenge is particularly acute in countries with fragmented governance structures or limited experience in managing large-scale environmental projects.

Another issue is that national strategies for sustainable development often face competition from short-term economic pressures, such as the need to repay existing debt or attract foreign investment. Governments may be tempted to shift priorities toward activities that promise immediate economic returns, such as extractive industries, agriculture, or tourism, which can undermine the long-term sustainability of conservation programs. Effective integration of debt-for-nature swaps into national development plans requires a strong political will to prioritize long-term environmental goals alongside short-term economic recovery.

How to Ensure Ongoing Financing for Conservation After the Swap

While debt-for-nature swaps can provide essential initial funding for conservation, the challenge remains to ensure ongoing financing for these efforts after the debt relief has been granted. To achieve long-term sustainability, conservation projects funded by debt-for-nature swaps need to be supported by additional revenue streams and financial mechanisms.

1. Establishing Sustainable Financing Mechanisms

One of the most important ways to ensure ongoing financing for conservation is through the establishment of sustainable financing mechanisms. This includes setting up conservation trust funds that generate income over time through investments, fees, or other revenue-generating activities. Trust funds can be designed to provide long-term, stable financing for conservation efforts by using interest earned on the fund's principal to support ongoing projects. The creation of such funds requires careful planning to ensure they are adequately capitalized and managed effectively.

2. Leveraging Ecotourism and Other Revenue Streams

Ecotourism is another important source of funding for conservation projects, particularly in countries with rich biodiversity and attractive natural landscapes. By promoting sustainable tourism, countries can generate income while protecting their natural resources. Debt-for-nature swaps can help establish the infrastructure needed for ecotourism, such as national parks, protected areas, and sustainable tourism practices. The revenue generated through ecotourism can then be reinvested into further conservation efforts.

In addition to ecotourism, other revenue-generating mechanisms, such as carbon credits, biodiversity offset programs, or payments for ecosystem services, can help provide a continuous source of funding for conservation initiatives. These mechanisms can be particularly important in countries that have access to international markets for carbon credits or other environmental services.

3. Engaging the Private Sector

The private sector can also play a role in providing ongoing financing for conservation after the swap. Companies, particularly those with a vested interest in preserving natural resources, such as those in the extractive industries or agriculture, may be willing to invest in conservation efforts as part of their CSR programs. Furthermore, private investors may be interested in impact investing opportunities related to sustainable development or environmental conservation. By leveraging private sector involvement, governments and NGOs can ensure that conservation projects remain financially viable after the debt-for-nature swap has been completed.

4. International and Multilateral Support

In addition to domestic financing sources, ongoing international and multilateral support can help ensure that conservation efforts are sustained. International development banks, global environmental funds, and climate finance initiatives, such as the Green Climate Fund, may be able to provide additional funding for conservation projects initiated through debt-for-nature swaps. By coordinating with international financial institutions, debtor countries can access supplementary resources to maintain and expand conservation efforts over time.

In conclusion, ensuring the financial sustainability of debt-for-nature swaps requires careful planning and a multi-faceted approach. Adequate debt relief is critical to achieving long-term conservation goals, but the funds released must be supplemented by sustainable financing mechanisms. Integrating debt-for-nature swaps into broader national development strategies and leveraging diverse revenue streams, such as ecotourism, carbon credits, and private sector investment, will be key to ensuring the continued success of conservation efforts. By addressing these financial challenges, countries can ensure that the environmental benefits of debt-for-nature swaps are realized for years to come.

3.3 Monitoring and Measuring Success

Effective monitoring and evaluation are essential components of debt-for-nature swaps, ensuring that the environmental objectives of these agreements are met. However, assessing the success of these swaps can be challenging due to the complexity of environmental outcomes, the long-term nature of conservation efforts, and the difficulty of attributing specific environmental improvements to the funds released through debt reduction. This section explores the challenges in monitoring and measuring the success of debt-for-nature swaps, the tools available for assessing their effectiveness, and the importance of balancing short-term results with long-term sustainability.

Difficulty in Assessing Environmental Outcomes

One of the primary challenges in monitoring debt-for-nature swaps is the inherent difficulty of assessing environmental outcomes. Environmental change is often gradual, and the impacts of conservation projects funded by debt-for-nature swaps can take years or even decades to manifest. For instance, reforestation projects, habitat restoration, and biodiversity conservation efforts require long-term commitments, and their success may not be immediately apparent. This long time horizon complicates the process of measuring the direct impact of debt-for-nature swaps on environmental outcomes.

Additionally, many environmental outcomes are influenced by a wide range of factors beyond the conservation projects themselves. Climate change, agricultural expansion, illegal logging, and natural disasters can all affect ecosystems, making it difficult to isolate the specific impact of debt-for-nature swap funds on the environment. This complexity requires sophisticated methods for tracking and measuring the success of these projects, as well as a clear understanding of the factors that may be influencing environmental change.

Another challenge is that environmental metrics are often qualitative or subjective. While some aspects of conservation, such as forest cover or species populations, can be quantified, others, such as ecosystem health or the effectiveness of community engagement, may be harder to measure in a standardized way. The lack of universally agreed-upon metrics for success makes it difficult to create consistent, comparable assessments of the effectiveness of debt-for-nature swaps across different countries and projects.

Tools for Measuring the Effectiveness of Swaps

Despite these challenges, there are a variety of tools and methods that can be employed to measure the effectiveness of debt-for-nature swaps and the success of the conservation projects they fund. Some of the most widely used tools include GIS, satellite imagery, biodiversity assessments, and environmental indicators.

1. **GIS**

GIS technology is a powerful tool for monitoring environmental changes, such as land-use change, deforestation, or the expansion of protected areas. GIS allows for the collection, analysis, and visualization of spatial data, which can be used to track the success of conservation projects funded by debt-for-nature swaps. For example, GIS can be used to map areas that have been reforested, track changes in forest cover over time, or monitor the expansion of protected areas. These tools enable stakeholders to evaluate the progress of conservation efforts on a regional, national, or global scale and ensure that the funds are being allocated to areas where they will have the most significant impact.

2. **Satellite Imagery**

Satellite imagery is another essential tool for tracking the effectiveness of debt-for-nature swaps. High-resolution satellite images provide real-time data on land cover changes, such as deforestation or forest regeneration, and can be used to assess the condition of protected areas or monitor illegal activities like logging or mining. Satellite imagery can be particularly useful for monitoring large, remote areas where on-the-ground inspections are difficult or costly. The ability to access up-to-date, high-resolution images also enables quick responses to emerging threats, such as illegal land clearance or natural disasters.

3. **Biodiversity Assessments**

Biodiversity assessments are crucial for evaluating the success of conservation efforts funded through debt-for-nature swaps. These assessments involve monitoring the health of ecosystems, including species populations, habitat quality, and the diversity of flora and fauna. Monitoring biodiversity can help assess whether conservation projects are effectively preserving ecosystems and enhancing biodiversity. Indicators such as species richness, the presence of endangered species, and habitat quality are commonly used to measure the success of conservation efforts.

4. **Environmental Indicators**

Environmental indicators are metrics used to evaluate the health of ecosystems and track the progress of conservation projects. These indicators may include factors such as air and water quality, soil health, and carbon sequestration rates. By tracking these indicators, stakeholders can assess whether the environmental goals of debt-for-nature swaps are being met. These indicators are particularly important for projects that focus on ecosystem services, such as water regulation or carbon storage, as they provide tangible measures of environmental health and sustainability.

Balancing Short-Term Results with Long-Term Sustainability

Another critical aspect of monitoring debt-for-nature swaps is the need to balance short-term results with long-term sustainability. Many conservation projects funded through debt-for-nature swaps may show immediate, measurable results, such as the establishment of protected areas or the planting of trees. However, the true success of these projects often depends on their ability to sustain these gains over time. It is essential to recognize that environmental outcomes, such as ecosystem restoration or species recovery, often require years or decades of consistent effort and long-term management to achieve meaningful results.

While short-term results are important for demonstrating the immediate impact of debt-for-nature swaps, it is crucial to focus on ensuring the long-term sustainability of these projects. This includes ensuring that conservation efforts are properly funded and managed beyond the initial debt relief period. Long-term sustainability requires ongoing monitoring, management, and investment, as well as the involvement of local communities in conservation efforts to ensure that projects are maintained and that the benefits are enduring.

Additionally, balancing short-term and long-term goals requires adjusting conservation strategies as new challenges arise. For example, climate change may introduce new pressures on ecosystems, requiring a shift in conservation priorities or methods.

The ability to adapt conservation strategies based on new data and evolving circumstances is essential for ensuring that debt-for-nature swaps continue to achieve their long-term environmental goals.

In conclusion, while monitoring and measuring the success of debt-for-nature swaps can be challenging, there are a variety of tools and methods available to assess their effectiveness. GIS, satellite imagery, biodiversity assessments, and environmental indicators can all play a role in tracking the progress of conservation projects and ensuring that funds are being used appropriately. Additionally, balancing short-term results with long-term sustainability is crucial for achieving lasting environmental outcomes. Effective monitoring and evaluation processes help ensure that debt-for-nature swaps deliver real, measurable environmental benefits and continue to support conservation goals well into the future.

Chapter 4: Modern Approaches to Debt-for-Nature Swaps

As the world faces increasingly complex environmental and financial challenges, debt-for-nature swaps have evolved to incorporate new strategies and technologies. This chapter explores modern approaches to these financial agreements, highlighting how innovative partnerships, evolving financial instruments, and technological advancements are reshaping the way debt-for-nature swaps are structured and implemented. By examining these contemporary methods, we can better understand how debt-for-nature swaps are adapting to address the global issues of climate change, biodiversity loss, and sustainable development in the 21st century.

4.1 Evolving Strategies and Partnerships

Debt-for-nature swaps have evolved significantly in recent years, adapting to changing global environmental and economic landscapes. Modern swaps involve an increasingly complex network of stakeholders, with a shift towards multi-stakeholder involvement and the integration of new financial mechanisms. These developments have broadened the scope of debt-for-nature swaps, allowing them to address not only sovereign debt issues but also broader sustainability goals, such as climate change mitigation, biodiversity preservation, and sustainable development. This section examines the key shifts in debt-for-nature swap strategies, including the growing role of public-private partnerships, international cooperation, and multilateral institutions, as well as the integration of modern financial tools like green bonds and climate finance into these agreements.

Shifts Towards Multi-Stakeholder Involvement

Traditionally, debt-for-nature swaps were negotiated between debtor countries and creditors, with environmental organizations often playing a secondary role. However, in recent years, there has been a significant shift towards multi-stakeholder involvement, involving a more diverse array of partners from both the public and private sectors. This shift reflects the increasing recognition that complex environmental challenges, such as biodiversity loss and climate change, require the collaboration of various stakeholders with different expertise and resources.

1. Public-Private Partnerships (PPPs)

One of the most significant developments in modern debt-for-nature swaps has been the rise of PPPs. These partnerships involve collaboration between governments, private sector companies, and environmental NGOs to fund and implement conservation projects. PPPs have become an essential part of debt-for-nature swaps because they bring together the financial resources of the private sector with the environmental expertise and on-the-ground knowledge of NGOs and governmental agencies. Through these partnerships, debt-for-nature swaps are able to access a broader range of financial resources, while also leveraging the private sector's innovation and efficiency in managing conservation efforts.

For example, private companies, particularly those in industries reliant on natural resources like agriculture, forestry, and extractive industries, have a vested interest in supporting sustainable resource management and environmental conservation. By participating in debt-for-nature swaps, these companies can help offset the environmental impact of their operations, enhance their corporate social responsibility profiles, and contribute to long-term sustainability goals. This growing private sector involvement has made debt-for-nature swaps more financially viable and capable of scaling up to address broader environmental issues.

2. International Cooperation

Another important trend in modern debt-for-nature swaps is the increasing role of international cooperation. The complexities of global environmental challenges, such as climate change and biodiversity loss, demand coordinated action across borders. International cooperation in debt-for-nature swaps has expanded beyond bilateral agreements to include multilateral organizations and cross-border initiatives. For instance, international financial institutions, such as the World Bank, regional development banks, and the International Monetary Fund (IMF), now play an active role in facilitating debt-for-nature swaps, providing technical assistance, and helping to structure deals that align with both environmental and financial goals.

Moreover, international agreements, such as the Paris Agreement on climate change, have created new opportunities for countries to engage in cross-border conservation projects. These agreements often involve commitments from multiple nations to jointly address shared environmental challenges, creating a framework in which debt-for-nature swaps can be implemented in a coordinated and effective manner. By integrating debt-for-nature swaps into broader international frameworks, these initiatives can gain greater legitimacy, attract more funding, and achieve more widespread environmental benefits.

Role of Multilateral Institutions and Environmental NGOs in Shaping Modern Swaps

Multilateral institutions and environmental NGOs have played a pivotal role in shaping modern debt-for-nature swaps, bringing their expertise, resources, and credibility to the table. Their involvement is key to ensuring that swaps align with international environmental and development goals while also maintaining financial viability and sustainability.

1. Multilateral Institutions

Multilateral institutions, such as the World Bank, the United Nations, and regional development banks, have been instrumental in advancing the concept of debt-for-nature swaps. These institutions provide the technical and financial support needed to structure complex deals, facilitate negotiations, and ensure that the environmental objectives of the swaps are aligned with broader sustainable development goals. For example, the World Bank's involvement in debt-for-nature swaps has helped to establish standardized procedures for structuring these agreements and ensuring that funds are effectively managed.

In addition to providing financial expertise, multilateral institutions also help align debt-for-nature swaps with global initiatives like the SDGs and the Convention on Biological Diversity. By working with debtor countries to integrate environmental conservation into national development plans, these institutions help ensure that debt-for-nature swaps contribute to long-term sustainability. Moreover, the involvement of multilateral institutions adds legitimacy to debt-for-nature swaps, making them more attractive to potential private sector partners and international creditors.

2. Environmental NGOs

Environmental NGOs have long been central to the success of debt-for-nature swaps, providing on-the-ground expertise and helping to design and implement conservation programs. In modern swaps, NGOs play an expanded role in not only monitoring and evaluating conservation efforts but also in facilitating multi-stakeholder partnerships and ensuring that the funds are allocated to projects that achieve measurable environmental outcomes.

NGOs also act as intermediaries between the debtor country, the creditor, and other stakeholders, ensuring that the environmental goals of the swap align with national priorities and that the funds are used transparently. In many cases, NGOs also provide technical assistance for the implementation of conservation projects, including biodiversity monitoring, habitat restoration, and sustainable land management practices. Their involvement is critical in ensuring that the environmental objectives of debt-for-nature swaps are met, and that the long-term sustainability of conservation projects is ensured.

Integration of Debt-for-Nature Swaps into Broader Financial Mechanisms Like Green Bonds and Climate Finance

In recent years, debt-for-nature swaps have increasingly been integrated into broader financial mechanisms, such as green bonds and climate finance, to expand their impact and attract additional resources for conservation. This integration reflects the growing recognition that environmental sustainability cannot be achieved through isolated financial instruments and that comprehensive, innovative financial solutions are needed to address the urgent challenges of biodiversity loss and climate change.

1. Green Bonds

Green bonds have become an important financial tool for supporting environmental conservation projects, and their integration into debt-for-nature swaps is an emerging trend. Green bonds are debt securities issued to raise capital specifically for environmentally friendly projects, such as renewable energy, climate adaptation, and conservation. By linking debt-for-nature swaps to green bonds, countries can access new sources of capital for environmental protection, while also ensuring that conservation projects are funded in a way that aligns with global environmental standards and goals.

The use of green bonds in debt-for-nature swaps allows governments and NGOs to raise additional funding for conservation initiatives, reducing the reliance on traditional debt relief alone. This can be particularly important for large-scale projects, such as forest preservation, that require sustained funding over time. Additionally, green bonds can attract private sector investors who are interested in supporting environmental sustainability, further expanding the pool of available resources.

2. Climate Finance

Climate finance has also become a key component of modern debt-for-nature swaps. As the world grapples with the impacts of climate change, international climate finance mechanisms, such as the Green Climate Fund (GCF), have emerged to support developing countries in mitigating and adapting to climate change. Debt-for-nature swaps are increasingly being integrated into these climate finance mechanisms, allowing countries to use the funds freed from debt relief to implement climate adaptation projects, such as sustainable agriculture, water management, and ecosystem-based adaptation.

By linking debt-for-nature swaps to climate finance, countries can address both the immediate financial pressures of sovereign debt and the long-term impacts of climate change. This integration not only provides additional funding for conservation but also ensures that these projects contribute to global climate goals, such as reducing greenhouse gas emissions and building climate resilience.

In conclusion, modern debt-for-nature swaps have evolved from simple debt reduction agreements into multifaceted, multi-stakeholder initiatives that leverage new financial mechanisms, international cooperation, and private sector involvement. The shift towards public-private partnerships and the growing role of multilateral institutions and environmental NGOs have expanded the scope and impact of these swaps, allowing them to address a broader range of environmental and development challenges. By integrating debt-for-nature swaps into global financial mechanisms like green bonds and climate finance, these initiatives are better positioned to secure long-term funding and contribute to global sustainability goals.

4.2 Technological Advancements in Debt-for-Nature Swaps

Technological advancements have significantly transformed the landscape of debt-for-nature swaps, enhancing their effectiveness in monitoring, managing, and ensuring the long-term success of conservation projects. Modern technologies such as GIS, satellite imagery, blockchain, and digital platforms play critical roles in providing real-time data, ensuring transparency, and engaging multiple stakeholders in the process. This section explores the key technological innovations that are reshaping debt-for-nature swaps, including the use of GIS and satellite technology for monitoring conservation areas, blockchain technology for ensuring transparency and accountability, and digital platforms for engaging stakeholders and tracking outcomes.

Use of GIS and Satellite Technology for Monitoring Conservation Areas

GIS and satellite technology are increasingly being used in debt-for-nature swaps to monitor conservation areas and track the effectiveness of funded projects. These technologies allow for real-time monitoring of large, often remote, conservation areas, providing key data that helps ensure that funds are being spent appropriately and that conservation objectives are being met.

1. GIS

GIS technology is widely used for mapping and analyzing spatial data, making it an essential tool for managing conservation areas funded by debt-for-nature swaps. With GIS, stakeholders can track changes in land use, monitor the expansion of protected areas, and identify regions at risk from deforestation or illegal activity. For example, GIS enables conservationists to visualize deforestation trends, land degradation, or biodiversity hotspots, providing valuable information for making strategic decisions about resource allocation and project priorities.

GIS allows for the integration of various data sets, such as satellite imagery, environmental variables, and community input, into a comprehensive analysis of conservation efforts. It can also be used to assess the impact of conservation activities on surrounding landscapes, such as the effect of forest restoration on soil erosion, water quality, or local biodiversity. The ability to create detailed, interactive maps also enhances the capacity to engage stakeholders, including governments, NGOs, and local communities, in the planning and implementation of conservation projects.

Moreover, GIS can help evaluate the progress of debt-for-nature swap initiatives by tracking environmental indicators over time. For instance, by comparing pre- and post-conservation data, stakeholders can assess whether conservation objectives are being met, such as increases in wildlife populations, restoration of ecosystems, or reductions in land-use change.

2. Satellite Technology

Satellite imagery, often used in conjunction with GIS, provides an invaluable tool for monitoring large conservation areas remotely. High-resolution satellite images enable the tracking of changes in land cover, such as deforestation, reforestation, or the expansion of protected areas. Satellite imagery can be used to identify illegal logging, poaching, or encroachment, which are common threats to conservation efforts in many developing countries.

The use of satellites allows for regular, up-to-date data on conservation areas, which is especially important for monitoring regions that are difficult to access or monitor on the ground. This technology also facilitates early detection of environmental risks, enabling timely interventions. For instance, satellite imagery can reveal signs of environmental damage caused by natural disasters or illegal activities, allowing conservation organizations to respond quickly and mitigate further harm.

Furthermore, satellite technology is increasingly capable of providing more than just imagery; it is now equipped with sensors that can collect data on atmospheric conditions, temperature, and vegetation health. This allows for more precise monitoring of climate change impacts, such as shifts in vegetation types or changes in forest cover due to rising temperatures. The ability to integrate these various data types into a unified monitoring framework enhances the effectiveness of debt-for-nature swaps in achieving their long-term conservation goals.

Blockchain Technology for Ensuring Transparency and Accountability

Blockchain technology, primarily known for its application in cryptocurrency, is increasingly being applied to environmental finance and debt-for-nature swaps as a means of ensuring transparency, accountability, and traceability. Blockchain's decentralized, immutable ledger allows for secure and transparent tracking of financial transactions, making it an ideal tool for managing funds released through debt relief.

1. Transparency and Financial Tracking

In debt-for-nature swaps, one of the key concerns is ensuring that the funds freed from debt relief are allocated correctly and used for the intended conservation projects. Blockchain technology addresses this concern by providing a transparent and auditable record of all financial transactions. By using blockchain, stakeholders can track how funds flow from creditors to debtor countries and ultimately to conservation projects. Each transaction is recorded in a secure, immutable ledger, ensuring that all parties—governments, NGOs, and local communities—have access to the same information and can verify that funds are being used appropriately.

2. Reducing Fraud and Mismanagement

Blockchain's transparency and security features also help reduce the risk of fraud, corruption, or mismanagement of funds. By recording each transaction in a public ledger, blockchain makes it difficult for any party to manipulate or divert funds without detection. This is particularly important in countries with weak governance or where financial oversight may be lacking. The use of blockchain technology can instill confidence among donors, creditors, and other stakeholders that funds are being used effectively for conservation.

3. Smart Contracts

Blockchain can also be used to implement smart contracts, which are self-executing agreements with the terms of the contract directly written into code. In the context of debt-for-nature swaps, smart contracts can be used to automate the disbursement of funds when certain conditions are met, such as the successful completion of specific conservation milestones. This automation ensures that funds are disbursed only when agreed-upon environmental goals have been achieved, helping to ensure that conservation projects remain on track and within budget.

Digital Platforms for Engaging Stakeholders and Tracking Outcomes

Digital platforms have become an essential tool for engaging stakeholders and ensuring that the objectives of debt-for-nature swaps are met. These platforms facilitate communication and collaboration between governments, NGOs, the private sector, and local communities, enabling more effective planning, implementation, and monitoring of conservation projects.

1. Stakeholder Engagement

Digital platforms allow for the participation of multiple stakeholders in the decision-making process and ensure that all parties are informed about the progress of debt-for-nature swap initiatives. For example, online platforms can be used to share real-time data on conservation projects, provide updates on project milestones, and solicit feedback from local communities and other stakeholders. These platforms can also serve as a space for NGOs and government agencies to collaborate, share best practices, and report on the outcomes of conservation projects.

Engaging stakeholders through digital platforms also allows for better community involvement in conservation efforts. Local communities are often the most directly affected by conservation initiatives and have valuable knowledge about the local environment. Digital platforms provide a means for communities to voice their concerns, offer insights, and participate in the management of conservation projects, ensuring that initiatives are locally relevant and widely supported.

2. **Real-Time Tracking and Reporting**

Digital platforms enable real-time tracking of project outcomes and financial flows, making it easier to monitor the progress of conservation efforts and assess their impact. By integrating GIS, satellite imagery, and blockchain, digital platforms can provide a comprehensive view of conservation projects, allowing stakeholders to track both financial and environmental data in one central location. This centralized approach helps ensure that everyone involved in the swap has access to accurate, up-to-date information, reducing the risk of miscommunication and improving project management.

3. **Data-Driven Decision Making**

By using digital platforms to collect and analyze data, stakeholders can make more informed decisions about the direction of conservation projects. These platforms can integrate data from multiple sources, including satellite imagery, field reports, and financial records, to provide a holistic view of the project's progress. Data-driven decision-making ensures that conservation efforts are continually optimized based on real-world conditions, helping to address challenges as they arise and maximize the impact of debt-for-nature swaps.

In conclusion, technological advancements have become an integral part of modern debt-for-nature swaps, enhancing the ability to monitor conservation areas, ensure transparency, and engage stakeholders in the conservation process. GIS and satellite technology provide real-time data for monitoring environmental outcomes, while blockchain ensures transparency and accountability in financial transactions. Digital platforms allow for better stakeholder engagement and provide a means to track outcomes effectively. By incorporating these technologies, debt-for-nature swaps are better equipped to address the complexities of environmental conservation, ensuring that funds are used efficiently and that conservation goals are achieved.

4.3 Incorporating Climate Change into Debt-for-Nature Agreements

As climate change increasingly becomes one of the most urgent global challenges, debt-for-nature swaps have evolved to include climate-related goals alongside traditional environmental conservation objectives. These swaps, originally designed to address sovereign debt and biodiversity conservation, are now being adapted to contribute to climate change mitigation and adaptation efforts. By linking debt relief to climate goals, debt-for-nature swaps offer a unique opportunity to support countries in their efforts to meet both their environmental and financial obligations. This section explores how debt-for-nature swaps can be used to fund climate change mitigation and adaptation, align with international climate agreements, and incorporate climate-related projects into these agreements.

How Debt-for-Nature Swaps Can Be Used to Fund Climate Change Mitigation and Adaptation

Debt-for-nature swaps can be powerful tools for financing climate change mitigation and adaptation projects, particularly in developing countries that are most vulnerable to the impacts of climate change. These swaps, by reducing a country's sovereign debt burden, free up financial resources that can be redirected toward climate action. The funds released through debt relief can be used to support a variety of climate-related initiatives, including the protection and restoration of carbon sinks, the implementation of sustainable agricultural practices, and the construction of climate-resilient infrastructure.

1. Climate Change Mitigation

Debt-for-nature swaps can play a critical role in climate change mitigation by directing funds towards projects that reduce greenhouse gas emissions and promote carbon sequestration. For instance, a significant portion of the funds can be used to finance reforestation, afforestation, and forest conservation programs, all of which help sequester carbon from the atmosphere. Forests act as crucial carbon sinks, absorbing CO_2 and mitigating the effects of climate change. Additionally, these funds can support sustainable land management practices, such as agroforestry or no-till agriculture, which can help reduce emissions from agriculture and improve soil health.

Swaps can also finance the development of renewable energy infrastructure, such as solar or wind power, in countries that are dependent on fossil fuels. By helping to transition to renewable energy sources, debt-for-nature swaps contribute directly to reducing carbon emissions and transitioning away from environmentally damaging energy practices.

2. Climate Change Adaptation

In addition to mitigation, debt-for-nature swaps can support climate adaptation efforts, particularly in countries that are already experiencing the impacts of climate change, such as rising sea levels, extreme weather events, and droughts. Adaptation projects typically involve making adjustments to infrastructure, agriculture, and natural systems to reduce vulnerability to climate impacts.

For example, funds released through debt-for-nature swaps can be used to finance the restoration of mangrove ecosystems, which provide coastal protection from storm surges and rising sea levels. Similarly, the funds can be used to implement water management systems that ensure communities have access to clean water in areas affected by droughts. Additionally, climate-resilient agricultural practices, such as the introduction of drought-resistant crops or improved irrigation systems, can help communities better cope with climate change impacts on food security.

Debt-for-nature swaps can also support disaster preparedness and response efforts, helping countries improve their resilience to extreme weather events like hurricanes, floods, and heatwaves. These projects often include strengthening infrastructure to withstand climate-related disasters, protecting vulnerable populations, and ensuring that ecosystems can continue to provide essential services despite changing conditions.

Aligning Debt-for-Nature Swaps with International Climate Agreements (Paris Agreement, SDGs)

The integration of climate change mitigation and adaptation into debt-for-nature swaps is not only beneficial for individual countries but also aligns with broader international climate and sustainability frameworks, such as the Paris Agreement and the United Nations SDGs. These global agreements set ambitious targets for reducing greenhouse gas emissions, increasing climate resilience, and promoting sustainable development, all of which can be supported by debt-for-nature swaps.

1. The Paris Agreement

The Paris Agreement, adopted in 2015, aims to limit global warming to well below 2°C above pre-industrial levels, with an emphasis on pursuing efforts to limit the temperature increase to 1.5°C. For developing countries, the transition to a low-carbon, climate-resilient future requires substantial financial investments in both mitigation and adaptation. Debt-for-nature swaps can help facilitate this transition by unlocking financial resources for climate action while simultaneously addressing sovereign debt challenges.

Debt-for-nature swaps can contribute to a country's Nationally Determined Contributions (NDCs) under the Paris Agreement by supporting the implementation of climate action plans. These actions may include the development of renewable energy infrastructure, the promotion of energy efficiency, and the adoption of climate-smart agriculture practices. By aligning debt-for-nature swaps with the targets outlined in the Paris Agreement, debtor countries can use the funds released from debt reduction to support their climate commitments.

2. The SDGs

The SDGs, adopted by the United Nations in 2015, include a specific goal (Goal 13) focused on climate action, as well as several other goals related to environmental sustainability, poverty reduction, and economic growth. Debt-for-nature swaps can help countries achieve multiple SDGs simultaneously by providing funding for conservation and climate adaptation projects that contribute to sustainable development.

For example, funds released through debt-for-nature swaps can be used to achieve SDG 15 (Life on Land) by supporting biodiversity conservation and ecosystem restoration efforts, which are essential for maintaining resilient ecosystems that can mitigate climate impacts. Similarly, by financing climate change adaptation projects, debt-for-nature swaps contribute to SDG 6 (Clean Water and Sanitation) and SDG 2 (Zero Hunger), which focus on ensuring access to water resources and food security in the face of climate change.

Aligning debt-for-nature swaps with the SDGs not only helps countries meet their international commitments but also ensures that debt relief is channeled toward projects that have a broad, lasting impact on both environmental sustainability and socio-economic development.

Incorporating Climate-Related Projects into Debt-for-Nature Agreements

Modern debt-for-nature swaps increasingly focus on climate-related projects, including both mitigation and adaptation efforts. These projects are designed to reduce a country's vulnerability to climate change while contributing to global climate goals. While specific case studies are not included here, it is important to recognize that these swaps are being used to support a wide range of climate-related initiatives.

1. Carbon Sequestration and Climate Resilience Projects

Many debt-for-nature swaps now incorporate carbon sequestration as a central focus. This includes the restoration of degraded forests, the creation of new protected areas, and the promotion of sustainable land management practices that enhance soil carbon storage. These projects not only mitigate climate change by reducing greenhouse gas concentrations but also increase the resilience of ecosystems and communities to climate impacts.

For example, countries with large forested areas are increasingly using debt-for-nature swaps to fund reforestation and afforestation projects. These efforts not only capture carbon but also help restore biodiversity, reduce soil erosion, and protect water resources, contributing to both climate change mitigation and broader environmental goals.

2. Climate-Resilient Infrastructure

In addition to natural climate solutions, modern debt-for-nature swaps are being used to finance climate-resilient infrastructure projects. This includes the construction of flood defenses, the strengthening of transportation networks to withstand extreme weather events, and the development of early warning systems for natural disasters. By integrating climate resilience into debt-for-nature swaps, countries can ensure that their infrastructure can withstand the impacts of climate change, while also addressing the immediate challenges of sovereign debt.

3. Sustainable Agriculture and Water Management

Another key area of focus in modern debt-for-nature swaps is sustainable agriculture and water management, which are critical for climate adaptation. These projects aim to improve food security and water access in regions affected by droughts, floods, and changing weather patterns. By promoting climate-smart agriculture techniques and efficient water use, debt-for-nature swaps help communities adapt to climate change while also reducing the environmental impact of agricultural practices.

In conclusion, incorporating climate change mitigation and adaptation into debt-for-nature swaps has become an essential strategy for addressing both the global climate crisis and the sovereign debt challenges faced by many developing countries. By aligning these swaps with international climate agreements like the Paris Agreement and the SDGs, they contribute to global efforts to combat climate change while also supporting sustainable development. Modern swaps are increasingly focused on climate-related projects, ranging from carbon sequestration to climate-resilient infrastructure, ensuring that the funds freed through debt relief are directed toward projects that not only conserve the environment but also build long-term resilience to climate change.

Chapter 5: The Future of Debt-for-Nature Swaps

As global environmental challenges continue to escalate, the need for innovative financial solutions like debt-for-nature swaps becomes more critical. This chapter explores the future of these agreements, examining how they can evolve to address emerging issues such as climate change, biodiversity loss, and sustainable development. It also looks at the potential for scaling up debt-for-nature swaps, integrating new financial mechanisms, and expanding their reach to include a wider range of stakeholders. By examining the future of debt-for-nature swaps, we can better understand their potential to contribute to long-term environmental and economic sustainability.

5.1 Expanding Debt-for-Nature Swaps Beyond Biodiversity

Debt-for-nature swaps have traditionally been focused on biodiversity conservation, primarily aimed at preserving ecosystems, reducing deforestation, and protecting endangered species. However, the increasing complexity of global environmental challenges has highlighted the need for these swaps to expand beyond biodiversity and address a wider range of sustainability issues. This expansion involves integrating environmental conservation into broader SDGs and leveraging debt-for-nature swaps to fund projects related to water security, food security, and renewable energy. This section explores how debt-for-nature swaps can be used to tackle these critical challenges and help create a more sustainable and resilient future.

Integrating Environmental Conservation into Broader Sustainable Development Goals

The SDGs, adopted by the United Nations in 2015, encompass a wide range of global challenges, including poverty reduction, clean water, climate action, and responsible consumption and production. While SDG 15 (Life on Land) focuses specifically on biodiversity, other SDGs are also deeply intertwined with environmental conservation. For instance, SDG 6 (Clean Water and Sanitation) and SDG 2 (Zero Hunger) are both directly related to sustainable water and food management, which are increasingly critical in addressing global environmental challenges.

Debt-for-nature swaps, traditionally focused on preserving ecosystems and protecting wildlife, can be expanded to fund initiatives that contribute to these broader sustainable development goals. By integrating conservation efforts into the broader SDG framework, debt-for-nature swaps can be designed to support projects that address multiple objectives simultaneously. For example, a swap could be structured to fund water conservation projects alongside biodiversity protection, addressing both SDG 6 and SDG 15 in tandem. Similarly, projects that promote sustainable agricultural practices can contribute to both SDG 2 and SDG 15, enhancing food security while protecting ecosystems.

This integrated approach requires a more holistic view of environmental conservation—one that goes beyond preserving biodiversity to encompass the broader environmental, social, and economic systems that support human well-being. Debt-for-nature swaps that integrate conservation with broader SDG objectives can generate more significant and lasting impacts, addressing interconnected issues like climate change, poverty, and resource depletion.

Addressing Water and Food Security through Debt-for-Nature Swaps

Water and food security are among the most pressing global challenges, particularly in developing countries that are heavily dependent on natural resources. Climate change, population growth, and unsustainable land management practices exacerbate these issues, threatening both access to clean water and the stability of global food systems. Given the close link between biodiversity and water and food security, debt-for-nature swaps offer an opportunity to tackle these challenges in an integrated way.

1. Water Security

Water scarcity is one of the most urgent threats facing many regions, especially in arid and semi-arid areas. Poor water management, deforestation, and climate change all contribute to declining water resources. Debt-for-nature swaps can help address water security by funding projects that focus on sustainable water management, watershed protection, and ecosystem restoration.

For instance, swaps can support the restoration of wetlands, forests, and river basins—ecosystems that play a crucial role in water filtration, storage, and regulation. By protecting these ecosystems, countries can improve both the quality and quantity of available water, benefiting local communities, agriculture, and biodiversity. Swaps can also fund projects that enhance water efficiency in agriculture, ensuring that irrigation practices are sustainable and that water is used more effectively, which can help secure food supplies and protect water resources for future generations.

Additionally, debt-for-nature swaps could be structured to support the development of water infrastructure that increases access to safe drinking water, particularly in areas affected by droughts or water shortages. These projects could include the construction of reservoirs, desalination plants, or rainwater harvesting systems, contributing to SDG 6 (Clean Water and Sanitation) while also supporting broader conservation goals.

2. Food Security

Food security is another critical challenge that can be addressed through debt-for-nature swaps. Agriculture is heavily dependent on healthy ecosystems, including soil fertility, water availability, and biodiversity. However, unsustainable agricultural practices, such as deforestation, overgrazing, and excessive use of chemical fertilizers, are damaging the environment and undermining food production systems.

Debt-for-nature swaps can be used to fund sustainable agricultural practices that improve soil health, increase crop resilience to climate change, and reduce environmental impacts. Projects could focus on agroforestry, organic farming, crop diversification, and soil conservation techniques that enhance food security while preserving ecosystems. These initiatives help to reduce the environmental footprint of agriculture, maintain biodiversity, and improve long-term food production capacity.

By integrating food security into debt-for-nature swaps, countries can ensure that conservation efforts also support the agricultural needs of local communities. This approach can help make food systems more resilient to climate change and more sustainable over the long term, contributing to SDG 2 (Zero Hunger).

Potential for Using Swaps to Fund Renewable Energy Projects

As the world transitions to a low-carbon economy, renewable energy has become a critical component of sustainable development. The energy sector is one of the largest contributors to greenhouse gas emissions, and shifting towards clean energy sources like wind, solar, and hydropower is essential for meeting global climate goals. Debt-for-nature swaps can be expanded to fund renewable energy projects, offering an opportunity to reduce both sovereign debt and carbon emissions simultaneously.

1. Financing Renewable Energy Infrastructure

Debt-for-nature swaps can provide the necessary capital to invest in renewable energy infrastructure in developing countries, which often lack the financial resources to make the transition to clean energy. These swaps could support the construction of solar farms, wind energy projects, and hydropower plants, which have the potential to provide clean, reliable energy to rural and off-grid communities.

By financing renewable energy projects, debt-for-nature swaps can help reduce dependence on fossil fuels, lower greenhouse gas emissions, and improve energy access in underserved regions. In many countries, the energy sector is one of the largest sources of emissions, and shifting to renewable energy is essential to meeting national and global climate targets.

2. **Decentralized and Community-Based Energy Solutions**

In addition to large-scale renewable energy projects, debt-for-nature swaps could also support decentralized and community-based energy solutions, such as solar-powered microgrids or biogas production. These smaller, locally tailored projects can be particularly effective in rural areas that are not connected to national energy grids. By empowering local communities to generate their own clean energy, these projects help build resilience to climate change and improve energy access while promoting environmental sustainability.

3. **Integrating Renewable Energy with Conservation Efforts**

Renewable energy projects funded by debt-for-nature swaps could also be integrated with conservation efforts. For example, solar or wind energy projects could be established in areas where traditional energy sources, such as fossil fuels or biomass, have led to environmental degradation. By shifting to cleaner energy sources, these projects not only reduce carbon emissions but also alleviate the pressures on natural resources, such as forests or wetlands, that are often used for fuel.

In conclusion, expanding debt-for-nature swaps to address water and food security, as well as renewable energy, presents an opportunity to tackle some of the world's most pressing sustainability challenges. By integrating these issues into debt-for-nature agreements, countries can address the interconnected environmental, economic, and social aspects of sustainable development. The flexibility of debt-for-nature swaps, combined with their ability to leverage debt relief for broader environmental goals, makes them a powerful tool for creating a more sustainable and resilient future. By using debt-for-nature swaps to finance water, food, and energy projects, nations can take a holistic approach to development that ensures long-term environmental protection and socio-economic stability.

5.2 Policy Recommendations for Enhancing the Impact of Debt-for-Nature Swaps

As debt-for-nature swaps evolve to address an increasingly complex range of global challenges, there is a growing need to enhance their design, implementation, and global coordination. These financial instruments offer substantial benefits, including debt relief and environmental conservation, but their full potential remains untapped due to various challenges in their structure and application. This section presents key policy recommendations aimed at improving the design and implementation of debt-for-nature swaps, expanding eligibility criteria to allow more countries to benefit, and strengthening international cooperation and institutional frameworks to increase the effectiveness of these initiatives.

Improving the Design and Implementation of Swaps

One of the primary challenges with debt-for-nature swaps is ensuring that they are effectively designed and implemented to achieve the intended environmental and financial outcomes. The design phase of these agreements often requires careful negotiation between debtor countries, creditors, and environmental organizations to ensure that the financial and environmental goals are aligned. However, there are opportunities to improve how these swaps are structured and how the conservation projects are implemented.

1. Aligning Debt Reduction with Long-Term Conservation Goals

To improve the impact of debt-for-nature swaps, it is essential to ensure that the amount of debt forgiven is proportional to the long-term costs of conservation. Many swaps currently only address immediate debt relief, leaving long-term conservation efforts underfunded. Policymakers should consider structuring debt-for-nature swaps to provide long-term financial sustainability for conservation projects, ensuring that adequate funds are allocated for monitoring, management, and scaling of these initiatives. This could include setting up conservation trust funds with clear investment strategies that generate ongoing returns, ensuring that funding for conservation does not cease once the initial debt relief is granted.

Additionally, swaps should be designed to allow for flexibility in addressing evolving environmental challenges. Climate change, biodiversity loss, and changing socio-economic conditions require adaptive management approaches. By incorporating flexibility into debt-for-nature swap agreements, such as allowing for the reallocation of funds if necessary, countries can ensure that conservation projects remain responsive to shifting environmental and developmental priorities.

2. Improving Monitoring and Evaluation

Robust monitoring and evaluation systems are critical to ensuring the success of debt-for-nature swaps. Governments and NGOs involved in debt-for-nature swaps must have clear, measurable targets for environmental outcomes and should regularly assess the effectiveness of conservation projects. Policymakers should develop standardized metrics for monitoring the impact of these swaps on biodiversity, carbon sequestration, water quality, and other environmental indicators. Third-party audits and independent evaluations should also be integrated into the design to ensure transparency and accountability in the use of funds.

Strengthening monitoring systems will not only improve the accountability of debt-for-nature swaps but also help identify successful strategies that can be scaled up or adapted to different contexts. These evaluations should consider both the environmental impact and the socio-economic benefits of conservation initiatives, ensuring that the projects contribute to sustainable development and address local community needs.

Expanding Eligibility Criteria for Debt-for-Nature Swaps

Currently, debt-for-nature swaps are primarily available to developing countries with significant debt burdens and rich biodiversity. While these criteria have been effective in addressing the needs of certain countries, expanding the eligibility for debt-for-nature swaps could increase the global impact of these initiatives, especially as environmental challenges such as climate change and biodiversity loss become more widespread.

1. Incorporating Middle-Income Countries

Most debt-for-nature swaps have been focused on low-income countries, but middle-income countries (MICs) also face substantial environmental challenges and sovereign debt issues. These countries often have significant biodiversity and are crucial to global efforts to mitigate climate change, yet they may not meet the current eligibility criteria for debt-for-nature swaps. Expanding the criteria to include MICs would allow a greater number of countries to benefit from debt relief and funding for environmental protection. Given the growing environmental pressures in these nations, such an expansion could lead to more effective global conservation efforts, as MICs are often home to large, ecologically significant ecosystems.

2. Including Countries with Climate Vulnerabilities

As climate change accelerates, countries that are not necessarily biodiversity-rich but are highly vulnerable to its impacts, such as small island nations or climate-affected regions, should also be considered for debt-for-nature swaps. These countries often face dire economic conditions due to the costs of climate adaptation and disaster response. Debt-for-nature swaps could help these nations finance climate resilience projects, such as strengthening coastal protections, enhancing water security, and restoring ecosystems that protect against natural disasters. By broadening eligibility to include climate-vulnerable countries, debt-for-nature swaps can support global climate adaptation and resilience efforts.

3. Addressing Debt Sustainability in Emerging Economies

Another potential avenue for expanding eligibility involves emerging economies facing high debt burdens that are not directly related to biodiversity or environmental concerns but still need financial solutions. Including these economies in debt-for-nature swaps could help them transition towards more sustainable development pathways by incorporating environmental goals alongside economic stabilization efforts. By targeting emerging economies with high levels of debt, debt-for-nature swaps can become a tool to encourage sustainable development practices and enhance global resilience.

Strengthening International Cooperation and Institutional Frameworks

International cooperation and strong institutional frameworks are essential for maximizing the impact of debt-for-nature swaps. Successful swaps require the collaboration of multiple stakeholders, including national governments, international creditors, environmental organizations, and local communities. Strengthening these cooperative efforts is key to ensuring that swaps are implemented effectively and achieve their long-term environmental and financial goals.

1. Enhancing Multilateral Support

Debt-for-nature swaps have traditionally been negotiated between bilateral creditors and debtor countries, but multilateral institutions such as the World Bank, the United Nations, and regional development banks have the potential to play a larger role in supporting these agreements. Policymakers should work to enhance the involvement of multilateral financial institutions in debt-for-nature swaps, ensuring that these institutions provide technical assistance, facilitate negotiations, and help manage the funds for conservation projects. Multilateral cooperation can also help coordinate swaps across countries and regions, maximizing their impact and aligning them with broader global sustainability goals, such as the SDGs and the Paris Agreement.

2. Strengthening Partnerships with the Private Sector

As public-sector funding for debt-for-nature swaps may be limited, expanding partnerships with the private sector can help increase the financial resources available for conservation. CSR programs, impact investments, and sustainability initiatives from multinational corporations can provide significant funding for conservation projects. Policymakers should encourage private sector involvement in debt-for-nature swaps by offering incentives, such as tax breaks or recognition for environmental contributions, which can make these investments more attractive. Furthermore, the private sector's expertise in resource management, sustainability practices, and innovative technologies can help ensure the successful implementation of these initiatives.

3. Strengthening Local and Regional Governance

Debt-for-nature swaps require strong governance at the local and regional levels to ensure that the projects funded by these agreements are effectively managed and benefit the communities involved. Strengthening the capacity of local governments and institutions to manage conservation efforts is crucial to the success of these swaps. This may involve providing technical training, developing local expertise in sustainable resource management, and ensuring that local communities have a say in the planning and implementation of projects. Local participation not only ensures the success of conservation efforts but also helps build long-term ownership of these initiatives, ensuring that they continue to thrive after the debt-for-nature swap agreement has been concluded.

4. Global Policy Coordination

Lastly, international organizations should work towards creating a more coherent global policy framework for debt-for-nature swaps. This framework could include standardized rules and guidelines for the design and implementation of these agreements, which would help streamline negotiations and make it easier for countries to engage in swaps. Policymakers should also work to integrate debt-for-nature swaps into global discussions on climate finance, debt relief, and sustainable development, ensuring that they are seen as an integral part of the solution to global environmental and economic challenges.

In conclusion, enhancing the impact of debt-for-nature swaps requires improvements in their design, implementation, and global coordination. By broadening the eligibility criteria, incorporating more countries into these agreements, and strengthening international cooperation, debt-for-nature swaps can become a more powerful tool for addressing global sustainability challenges. Expanding partnerships with multilateral institutions, the private sector, and local communities, while also strengthening governance and accountability, will help ensure that these swaps achieve their full potential in promoting both environmental conservation and financial stability.

5.3 Scaling Up Debt-for-Nature Swaps Globally

Scaling up debt-for-nature swaps globally presents an opportunity to leverage this innovative financial tool to address both sovereign debt challenges and pressing environmental crises. However, achieving large-scale impact requires overcoming several obstacles, including financial constraints, political challenges, and a lack of infrastructure in many low-income countries. Expanding participation from diverse stakeholders, including the private sector and international investors, and utilizing new financial instruments and technology can help overcome these barriers and make debt-for-nature swaps a more widespread and effective solution. This section explores the challenges to scaling up debt-for-nature swaps, strategies for increasing private sector and investor participation, and the potential for new financial instruments and technological tools to enhance the effectiveness of these agreements.

Overcoming Challenges to Implementing Swaps in Low-Income Countries

Low-income countries often face the greatest barriers to implementing debt-for-nature swaps due to their limited financial resources, weaker institutional frameworks, and lack of technical expertise. Despite these challenges, debt-for-nature swaps offer an opportunity to address sovereign debt crises while simultaneously advancing conservation goals. To scale up these swaps in low-income countries, it is crucial to address the key obstacles that prevent successful implementation.

1. Financial Constraints and Debt Sustainability

One of the primary challenges in low-income countries is the overwhelming debt burden, which often prevents them from dedicating sufficient resources to environmental conservation. While debt-for-nature swaps can provide much-needed financial relief, the amount of debt that can be forgiven is typically limited to a portion of the country's overall debt. For countries with large debt burdens, this limited debt relief may not be sufficient to make a significant impact on environmental projects. To overcome this challenge, it may be necessary to combine debt-for-nature swaps with other forms of debt relief or concessional financing from international financial institutions. By incorporating these additional funding sources, low-income countries can scale up their conservation efforts while also addressing their broader economic needs.

2. Weak Institutional Frameworks and Governance

Effective implementation of debt-for-nature swaps requires strong institutional frameworks and governance structures. Many low-income countries, however, struggle with weak institutions, which can result in poor management of the funds freed from debt reduction or misallocation of resources. To ensure the success of debt-for-nature swaps, it is essential to build the capacity of local institutions, improve transparency, and create robust mechanisms for monitoring and reporting on conservation projects. This may involve providing technical assistance to help governments and NGOs manage conservation funds effectively, as well as developing clear guidelines for the disbursement of funds.

3. Political Stability and Governance

Political instability and frequent changes in government pose significant challenges to implementing long-term agreements like debt-for-nature swaps. In low-income countries, shifts in government priorities or the risk of political unrest can disrupt conservation projects and undermine the continuity of debt-for-nature agreements. Strengthening political stability and ensuring that conservation efforts are embedded in national development strategies are key to overcoming this challenge. Creating broad political support for debt-for-nature swaps, including from local communities, can help ensure that these initiatives have lasting political buy-in and are not subject to abrupt changes in policy.

Increasing Participation from the Private Sector and International Investors

To scale up debt-for-nature swaps, it is critical to increase participation from the private sector and international investors. These groups can provide additional capital and resources needed to fund large-scale conservation projects, expanding the scope and impact of debt-for-nature swaps. The private sector, in particular, has a vested interest in supporting environmental sustainability, as many industries rely on healthy ecosystems for their long-term viability.

1. **Private Sector Engagement through CSR**

Private companies, particularly those in sectors like agriculture, forestry, and mining, can play an important role in supporting debt-for-nature swaps through CSR programs. These companies are increasingly aware of the environmental risks associated with their operations and are seeking opportunities to mitigate their environmental impact. By participating in debt-for-nature swaps, companies can contribute to sustainable development goals while also enhancing their reputations and improving their environmental, social, and governance (ESG) performance. Policymakers should incentivize private sector participation by offering tax benefits, public recognition, or partnership opportunities with environmental organizations and international institutions.

2. **International Investors and Impact Funds**

International investors, particularly those focused on impact investing, have a significant role to play in scaling up debt-for-nature swaps. Impact investors seek to achieve both financial returns and positive environmental outcomes, making debt-for-nature swaps an attractive opportunity for these funds. The development of impact investing platforms and the creation of blended finance mechanisms, where public funds are used to de-risk private investments, can encourage international investors to participate in debt-for-nature swaps. By involving investors in these initiatives, low-income countries can access much-needed capital for conservation projects while ensuring that financial returns are reinvested into sustainable development goals.

3. **PPPs**

PPPs are another way to scale up debt-for-nature swaps by leveraging the financial resources and expertise of the private sector. In a PPP model, the government, private sector entities, and environmental organizations collaborate to fund and manage conservation projects. These partnerships can pool resources, reduce risks, and accelerate the implementation of large-scale environmental initiatives. PPPs also bring together a variety of stakeholders with different strengths and expertise, ensuring that conservation projects are more effectively planned, implemented, and managed.

Leveraging New Financial Instruments and Technology for Large-Scale Swaps

To scale up debt-for-nature swaps, it is important to leverage new financial instruments and technological tools that can increase efficiency, reduce risks, and expand the range of potential investments. These innovations can make debt-for-nature swaps more attractive to a wider range of stakeholders, including private investors, multilateral institutions, and governments.

1. Green Bonds and Climate Finance

Green bonds have emerged as an innovative financial instrument that can be integrated into debt-for-nature swaps. These bonds are specifically designed to fund environmentally sustainable projects, such as renewable energy, ecosystem restoration, and conservation initiatives. By issuing green bonds as part of a debt-for-nature swap, countries can access additional financing from international investors and use the funds to support large-scale environmental projects. The integration of green bonds with debt-for-nature swaps offers a way to diversify the funding sources for conservation while simultaneously advancing climate change goals.

2. Blended Finance Models

Blended finance is another approach to scaling up debt-for-nature swaps by combining public and private funding to reduce investment risks and attract more capital for conservation. Through blended finance models, governments and development institutions can de-risk debt-for-nature swaps by providing concessional finance or guarantees that make investments more attractive to private investors. This approach helps leverage private capital for conservation projects that may otherwise be seen as too risky or uncertain. By using blended finance mechanisms, debt-for-nature swaps can attract a wider range of investors, enabling larger and more impactful conservation projects.

3. Technological Innovations for Monitoring and Data Management

Advances in technology, particularly in the areas of satellite imagery, GIS mapping, and blockchain, have made it easier to track and monitor the impact of conservation projects funded through debt-for-nature swaps. These technologies provide real-time data on environmental changes, making it easier to assess the effectiveness of conservation initiatives and ensure that funds are being used efficiently. For instance, satellite technology allows for the monitoring of deforestation, land-use changes, and habitat degradation, providing clear evidence of the environmental impact of debt-for-nature swaps. Blockchain technology, meanwhile, can enhance transparency and reduce the risk of fraud or mismanagement by ensuring that funds are tracked and managed securely.

In conclusion, scaling up debt-for-nature swaps globally requires overcoming significant challenges, including financial constraints and institutional weaknesses in low-income countries. However, by increasing participation from the private sector and international investors, and leveraging new financial instruments and technologies, debt-for-nature swaps can be expanded to have a much larger impact on global conservation and sustainable development goals. The development of innovative financial mechanisms, such as green bonds and blended finance models, combined with technological advancements in monitoring and data management, will ensure that debt-for-nature swaps can be a key tool in addressing the world's environmental and financial crises.

Chapter 6: Conclusion and the Road Ahead

As debt-for-nature swaps continue to evolve, their potential to address both environmental degradation and sovereign debt crises remains immense. This chapter reflects on the key insights gained throughout the book, synthesizing the challenges, successes, and future opportunities for scaling up these innovative agreements. Looking ahead, we explore the necessary steps for enhancing the effectiveness of debt-for-nature swaps, strengthening global cooperation, and ensuring that these financial instruments play a pivotal role in achieving long-term sustainability and resilience for both people and the planet.

6.1 Key Insights

Debt-for-nature swaps have emerged as a powerful tool to address the dual challenges of sovereign debt crises and environmental degradation. This innovative financial instrument has the potential to both reduce a country's debt burden and simultaneously fund vital conservation projects, making it a key strategy in advancing global sustainability goals. Throughout this book, we have explored the evolution of debt-for-nature swaps, their mechanisms, and their expanding role in addressing pressing environmental and economic challenges. In this section, we summarize the main insights from the book and reflect on the importance of debt-for-nature swaps in achieving global sustainability.

Summary of the Book's Main Points

The book began by introducing the concept of debt-for-nature swaps, providing a comprehensive overview of how they work and their historical development. Initially, these agreements were focused on reducing sovereign debt while funding biodiversity conservation projects. Over time, however, their scope has expanded to address broader environmental issues, including climate change mitigation and adaptation, water and food security, and sustainable development.

The first chapters outlined the key principles and mechanisms involved in debt-for-nature swaps, explaining how debt forgiveness or purchase is exchanged for environmental commitments, often supported by international financial institutions and NGOs. These swaps function by directing funds saved from debt reduction into conservation projects, which are carefully managed and overseen to ensure that they meet both environmental and financial goals.

The book also delved into the stakeholders involved in debt-for-nature swaps, highlighting the roles played by governments, creditors, NGOs, multilateral organizations, and private sector partners. Each party brings valuable resources, expertise, and interests to the table, and their collaboration is critical for the success of these swaps.

A central theme of the book has been the challenges and opportunities associated with debt-for-nature swaps. While these agreements offer a promising solution for many countries, their effectiveness is often limited by political instability, weak institutional frameworks, and financial constraints. The book examined strategies for overcoming these challenges, such as increasing private sector participation, expanding eligibility criteria for swaps, and strengthening institutional frameworks for governance and accountability.

The latter chapters focused on the modern evolution of debt-for-nature swaps, exploring how technological advancements, such as satellite imagery, blockchain, and GIS, are revolutionizing the way these swaps are monitored and managed. By integrating these technologies, stakeholders can track the effectiveness of conservation projects in real time, ensuring that funds are used transparently and that the environmental outcomes are achieved.

Finally, the book highlighted the potential for debt-for-nature swaps to support broader sustainability goals, including climate change mitigation, water and food security, and the transition to renewable energy. The future of debt-for-nature swaps lies in their ability to evolve and adapt to meet the changing needs of global sustainability, positioning them as a key financial tool in achieving the United Nations SDGs.

Importance of Debt-for-Nature Swaps in Achieving Global Sustainability

Debt-for-nature swaps have become a critical tool in the global push toward sustainability. As sovereign debt burdens continue to rise, particularly in developing nations, debt-for-nature swaps offer a unique solution that aligns financial relief with environmental preservation. By redirecting funds that would otherwise go toward servicing debt, these agreements can finance conservation projects that mitigate climate change, protect biodiversity, and promote sustainable development.

The importance of debt-for-nature swaps extends beyond merely reducing financial liabilities. These swaps have the potential to create lasting environmental benefits, such as restoring ecosystems, protecting endangered species, and ensuring the sustainable management of natural resources. Furthermore, by incorporating climate change adaptation and mitigation into the framework of debt-for-nature swaps, these agreements contribute to global efforts to meet international climate targets, including the goals set out in the Paris Agreement.

Debt-for-nature swaps also promote resilience by enhancing local communities' ability to adapt to environmental changes. Conservation efforts funded through these swaps can help protect vital ecosystems, such as forests, wetlands, and coral reefs, which provide critical services like clean water, food, and flood protection. These ecosystems, in turn, support local economies and livelihoods, making debt-for-nature swaps an integral part of a broader strategy for poverty reduction and sustainable development.

Moreover, as the global community continues to focus on the SDGs, debt-for-nature swaps present an opportunity to leverage innovative financial mechanisms to address multiple global challenges simultaneously. These swaps offer a tangible solution for countries facing both economic difficulties and environmental degradation, helping to align their national development plans with global sustainability objectives.

In conclusion, debt-for-nature swaps represent a significant tool in achieving global sustainability. By combining debt relief with environmental conservation, they offer a win-win solution that addresses both financial and ecological challenges. With the right political will, institutional support, and multi-stakeholder involvement, debt-for-nature swaps can play a pivotal role in advancing the goals of the SDGs and ensuring a sustainable future for all.

6.2 Looking to the Future

The future of debt-for-nature swaps lies in their continued evolution as a critical tool for addressing both environmental and financial challenges. As global environmental issues intensify and sovereign debt burdens rise, debt-for-nature swaps are increasingly seen as a viable solution that can achieve multiple objectives—reducing debt, supporting conservation efforts, and advancing sustainable development. This section explores the evolving role of debt-for-nature swaps in international finance and the future opportunities for integrating environmental conservation into broader financial systems.

The Evolving Role of Debt-for-Nature Swaps in International Finance

Debt-for-nature swaps have evolved significantly since their inception, and their role in international finance is likely to continue expanding. Initially, these swaps were primarily seen as a way for countries to reduce sovereign debt while simultaneously supporting biodiversity conservation. Today, however, they are increasingly integrated into broader strategies for climate change mitigation, sustainable development, and poverty reduction.

One of the key developments in the evolution of debt-for-nature swaps is the growing recognition of their potential to address global environmental crises, particularly climate change and biodiversity loss. As international financial institutions, such as the World Bank, the IMF, and the United Nations, emphasize the need for innovative financial solutions to achieve the SDGs, debt-for-nature swaps are becoming an essential part of the financial landscape. These swaps allow countries to reduce their debt burden while also investing in projects that contribute to global sustainability.

Additionally, debt-for-nature swaps are increasingly viewed as a tool to enhance global cooperation. As countries and international organizations work together to tackle shared environmental challenges, such as climate change and resource depletion, debt-for-nature swaps provide a mechanism for creating win-win solutions. By reducing debt and supporting environmental conservation, these swaps contribute to both the economic stability of debtor countries and the protection of the global commons.

Another important trend is the growing involvement of the private sector in debt-for-nature swaps. As companies, particularly those with environmental footprints, face increasing pressure to address their sustainability impacts, they are recognizing the value of contributing to conservation efforts. Debt-for-nature swaps provide a way for private investors and corporations to fulfill their CSR commitments, improve their ESG profiles, and support large-scale environmental projects. The private sector's growing involvement will help scale up debt-for-nature swaps and broaden their impact.

Future Opportunities for Integrating Environmental Conservation into Financial Systems

As the world moves toward a more sustainable financial future, integrating environmental conservation into global financial systems presents significant opportunities. Debt-for-nature swaps are just one example of how financial instruments can be used to advance environmental goals, and there is considerable potential for these agreements to be integrated into broader financial strategies.

1. Green Finance and Sustainable Investment

One of the most promising areas for future growth in debt-for-nature swaps is the expanding field of green finance. Green bonds, sustainable investment funds, and other financial instruments focused on environmental sustainability are gaining popularity as investors seek to support projects that promote climate resilience, biodiversity, and sustainable resource management. Debt-for-nature swaps can be linked to green finance initiatives, where the funds freed by debt reduction are channeled into green infrastructure projects, renewable energy, and conservation. By integrating debt-for-nature swaps into green finance markets, countries can access more funding options while contributing to global environmental goals.

2. Blended Finance Models

Blended finance, which combines concessional funding with private investment, is another area where debt-for-nature swaps can play a significant role. By using blended finance models, governments and multilateral institutions can leverage private capital for conservation projects, making them more scalable and attractive to investors. Debt-for-nature swaps can be integrated into blended finance frameworks, where private sector investments are paired with public sector funding to reduce financial risks and ensure the long-term sustainability of conservation projects. This approach helps expand the pool of resources available for environmental protection while reducing the dependency on public funds.

3. Carbon Markets and Climate Finance

As global markets for carbon credits and climate finance continue to grow, debt-for-nature swaps can be linked to carbon offsetting programs. By supporting projects that enhance carbon sequestration—such as forest conservation and reforestation—debt-for-nature swaps can help generate carbon credits that can be sold in international carbon markets. This would provide a new revenue stream for conservation projects, making them financially self-sustaining. By aligning debt-for-nature swaps with carbon markets and climate finance initiatives, countries can contribute to global efforts to mitigate climate change while also addressing their debt issues.

4. Ecosystem-Based Solutions and Resilient Economies

The future of debt-for-nature swaps lies in integrating ecosystem-based solutions into broader financial systems. This includes leveraging natural capital—such as forests, wetlands, and oceans—to support sustainable economic development. Debt-for-nature swaps that focus on protecting or restoring these ecosystems can help build resilience to climate change, improve disaster preparedness, and ensure the long-term availability of ecosystem services. By mainstreaming ecosystem-based approaches into financial systems, debt-for-nature swaps can play a central role in building more resilient and sustainable economies.

In conclusion, the evolving role of debt-for-nature swaps in international finance presents significant opportunities for scaling up these agreements and expanding their impact on global sustainability. By integrating environmental conservation into broader financial strategies, such as green finance, blended finance, and carbon markets, debt-for-nature swaps can become a key tool in addressing both environmental and economic challenges. As the global community increasingly focuses on sustainability, debt-for-nature swaps will play an integral role in ensuring that countries can achieve their conservation and development goals while managing their financial obligations. The future of these agreements is bright, with the potential to drive large-scale environmental impact and contribute to a more sustainable and resilient global economy.

www.ingramcontent.com/pod-product-compliance
Lightning Source LLC
Chambersburg PA
CBHW052141270326
41930CB00012B/2979